Instructor's Solutions Manual for

The Practice of Statistics

TI-83 Graphing Calculator Enhanced

Daniel S. Yates

W. H. Freeman and Company
New York

ISBN 0-7167-3571-7 (EAN: 9780716735717)

Printed in the United States of America

Fifth printing

W. H. Freeman and Company
41 Madison Avenue
New York, NY 10010

www.whfreeman.com

Contents

Preface

This Instructor's Solutions Manual contains the full solutions to all exercises in the text, *The Practice of Statistics: TI-83 Graphing Calculator Enhanced* (TPS). Most of these solutions were prepared by Professor Darryl K. Nester of Bluffton College. Professor Christopher E. Barat of Virginia State University assisted me in preparing the balance of the solutions, particularly for those exercises that utilize the TI-83 graphing calculator. The significant contributions of Professors Nester and Barat are acknowledged with gratitude.

I welcome comments, suggestions for improvement of TPS and this Instructor's Solutions Manual, and reports of errors that escaped detection and can be fixed in new printings. You can reach me at:

Electronic Classroom
7053 Messer Road
Richmond, VA 23231
Tel: 804-226-8725
Fax: 804-236-3689
e-mail: dyates@pen.k12.va.us

Daniel S. Yates

Exploring Data

SECTION 1.1

1.1 (a) Male and female members of the class.
 (b) Two. Pulse rates, gender.
 (c) Pulse rate: beats per minute. Gender: male, female.
 (d) Pulse rate is quantitative; gender is categorical.

1.2 "Region" is categorical; all others are quantitative.

1.3 (a) categorical; (b) quantitative; (c) categorical; (d) categorical; (e) quantitative; (f) quantitative.

1.4

```
MTB > DotPlot 'DRPscore'.
```

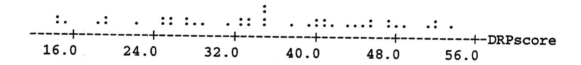

DRPscore   N =   44

Midpoint	Count	
15	3	
20	4	
25	6	
30	3	
35	8	
40	7	
45	7	
50	5	
55	1	

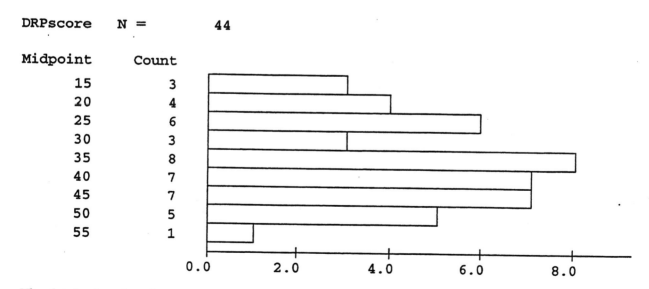

The dotplot has the advantage that it lets you see individual observations. The center of the distribution is 35, and there are approximately the same number of points to the left and right of the center. There are no major gaps or outliers. The distribution is approximately symmetric. This is confirmed by the histogram. The disadvantage of the histogram is that it doesn't show individual observations, and changing the centers and widths of the bars can dramatically change the general appearance of the histogram.

1.5 (a) Roughly symmetric, though it might be viewed as SLIGHTLY skewed to the right. (b) About 15%. (39% of the stocks had a total return less than 10%, while 60% had a return less than 20%. This places the center of the distribution somewhere between 10% and 20%.) (c) The smallest return was between −70% and −60%, while the largest was between 100% and 110%. (d) 23% (1 + 1 + 1 + 1 + 3 + 5 + 11).

1.6 (a) Skewed to the right; center at about 3 (31 less than 3, 11 equal to 3, 23 more than 3); spread: 0 to 10. No outliers. (b) About 23% (15 out of 65 years).

1.7 Lightning histogram: centered at noon (or more accurately, somewhere from 11:30 to 12:30). Spread is from 7 to 17 (or more accurately, 6:30 AM to 17:30, i.e., 5:30 PM). Shakespeare histogram: centered at 4, spread from 1 to 12.

1.8 (a) Table below. (b) Histogram below. Children (under 10) represent the single largest group in the population; about one out of five Americans was under 10 in 1950. There is a slight dip in the 10–19 bracket, then the percentages trail off gradually after that. (c) Histogram below. The projections show a much greater proportion in the higher age brackets — there is now a gradual rise in the proportion up to ages 40–49, followed by the expected decline in the proportion of "senior citizens."

(a)	Age group	1950	2075
	0–9	19.4%	11.2%
	10–19	14.4	11.5
	20–29	15.9	11.8
	30–39	15.1	12.3
	40–49	12.8	12.2
	50–59	10.3	12.1
	60–69	7.3	11.1
	70–79	3.6	8.8
	80–89	1.1	6.1
	90–99	0.1	2.5
	100–109	0.0	0.5

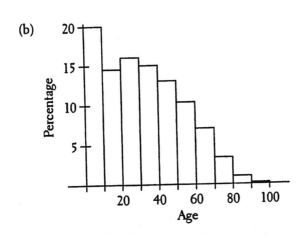

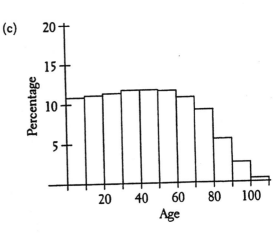

1.9 Outlier: 200. Center: 137 to 140 (there are nine observations less than or equal to 137, and nine greater than or equal to 140). Spread (ignoring the outlier): 101 to 178.

```
10 | 139
11 | 5
12 | 669
13 | 77
14 | 08
15 | 244
16 | 55
17 | 8
18 |
19 |
20 | 0
```

1.10 (a) Stemplot below. (b) Distribution is skewed to the left, centered between 25 and 29 (the 10th and 11th scores). One might consider 10 to be an outlier, and possibly 15 as well. (c) 27 (or any score between 25 and 29).

```
1 | 0
1 | 5
2 | 0023344
2 | 59
3 | 000112223
```

1.11 Answers will vary, but your description should compare centers, spread, gaps, and outliers.

1.12 (a)

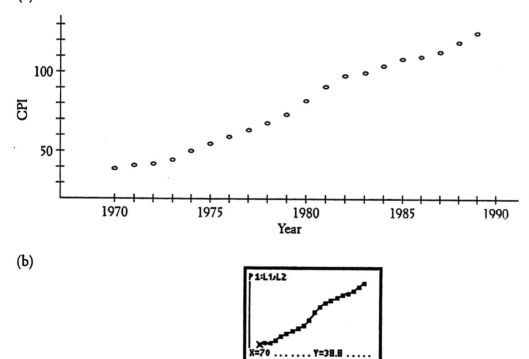

(b)

(c) Prices increased throughout the entire period. (d) Prices rose most quickly from 1979 to 1980, the steepest part of the graph. This was an increase of 9.8 units over one year, from the table. The slowest rise occurred from about 1970 to 1973, with a similar rate of increase in 1985 to 1986.

1.13 (a) Virginia Road Fatalities, 1986–1996: The graph shows a general decline over the decade. Possible reasons include safer, newer, and better cars; more airbags and antilock brakes; increased use of seat belts (estimated at 70%, there is a mandatory seat belt law in Virginia); newer and better roads with safer design engineering; law enforcement and educational groups promoting safe driving habits.

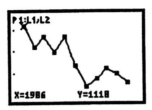

(b) Alcohol-related Fatalities, 1986–1995: Again, there appears to be a gradual decline in recent years. Possible reasons include those in (a), as well as better education on the dangers of drunk driving; a growing national intolerance of drunk driving; and stiffer penalties.

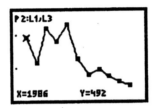

1.14 (a) The individuals are the company's employees. (b) The variables "Gender," "Race," and "Job Type" are categorical. (c) "Age" and "Salary" are quantitative, measured in years and dollars, respectively.

1.15 Slightly skewed to the right, centered at 4.

1.16 (a) Roughly symmetric (though with two apparent peaks). (b) The center (a "typical" batting average) is between .265 and .275, and the spread is from .185 to .355 (ignoring Brett).

1.17 (a)

```
Stem-and-leaf of Ruth     N = 15
Leaf Unit = 1.0
        1      2 2
        2      2 5
        3      3 4
        4      3 5
        6      4 11
       (5)     4 66679
        4      5 44
        2      5 9
        1      6 0
```

The distribution is slightly skewed to the left, and centered at 46. 60 is not an outlier. (b) Maris' 61 home-run year is an outlier—a clear departure from the other nine years. The bulk of Ruth's stemplot is numerically higher than Maris'. The center of Ruth's distribution (46) is substantially higher than the center of Maris' (32). Indeed, excluding the outlier, Ruth's four lowest years are at about the same level as Maris' best five years.

```
 8 | 0 |
43 | 1 |
 6 | 1 |
 3 | 2 | 2
86 | 2 | 5
 3 | 3 | 4
 9 | 3 | 5
   | 4 | 11
   | 4 | 66679
   | 5 | 44
   | 5 | 9
 1 | 6 | 0
```

1.18 (a) After rounding all numbers to the first place after the decimal and splitting stems, the plot shows the distribution to be fairly symmetric, with a high outlier of 4.7 (4.69). (b) The time plot shows no clear trend.

```
1 | 12
1 | 556799
2 | 0111122233
2 | 568899
3 | 0113
3 | 5
4 |
4 | 7
```

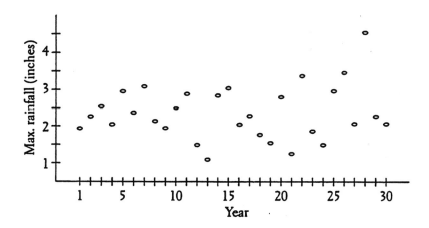

1.19 (a) Round to nearest integer before creating stemplot. (b) There is no particular observable shape (considering symmetry and skewness). (c) (Time plot on next page.) (d) The time plot shows an increasing trend—adjustments should be made to counteract the rising tensions.

```
25 | 7
26 | 5
27 | 00
28 | 034
29 | 7
30 | 58
31 | 08
32 | 78
33 | 69
34 | 033
35 |
36 |
37 | 5
```

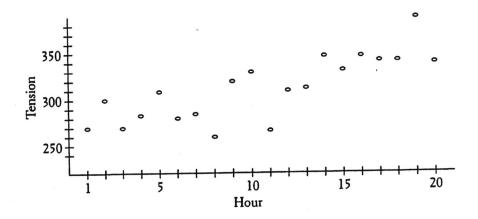

1.20 Shown below is one possible plot with a compressed time axis, so that it appears to be steeper than Figure 1.7. Plots that appear in newspapers or magazines may be "distorted" (stretched or compressed) in this way so that they fit into a particular space.

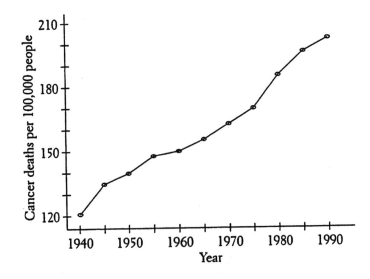

1.21 There are two distinct groups of states—"less than 30%" and "more than 40%." There are no particular outliers.

```
0 | 4
0 | 55566899
1 | 0001222234
1 | 567
2 | 024
2 | 58
3 |
3 |
4 | 2244
4 | 59
5 | 244
5 | 57889
6 | 0224
6 | 789
7 | 024
```

1.22 Stems are split *five* ways. The distribution seems to be skewed to the right.

```
2 | 23
2 | 4445
2 | 6666777
2 | 8888999999
3 | 01111
3 | 2222233333
3 | 55
3 | 66
3 | 8888
4 | 00
4 | 23
4 | 4
```

1.23 Skewed to the right. New Jersey (at $9,159 per student) might be considered outlier.

```
3 | 0233
3 | 67777
4 | 02234444
4 | 688889
5 | 0000112233334
5 | 56799
6 | 024
6 | 5
7 | 0
7 | 99
8 | 2
8 | 5
9 | 2
```

SECTION 1.2

1.24 (a) $n = 14$, $\Sigma x = 1190$. The mean is $\bar{x} = \dfrac{\Sigma x}{n} = \dfrac{1190}{14} = 85$

   (b) If the 15th score is 0, then $n = 15$, $\Sigma x = 1190$, and the new mean is

$$\bar{x} = \frac{\Sigma x}{n} = \frac{1190}{15} = 79.3$$

The fact that this value of $\bar{x}$ is less than 85 indicates the nonresistance property of $\bar{x}$. The extremely low outlier at 0 pulled the mean below 85.

   (c) Minitab splits the decades to show greater detail.

```
Stem-and-leaf of C1     N = 14
Leaf Unit = 1.0
   7    4
   7    568
   8    024
   8    67
   9    013
   9    68
```

And here is a histogram, with the widths of the bars specified to correspond to letter grades: D (68–75), C (76–83), B (84–91), and A (92–100). Both plots show a fairly balanced or symmetric distribution, with the histogram suggesting a slight skewness to the left. (Note that the mean and the median are the same (85).

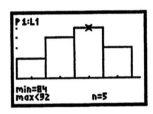

Given a rather small data set like this one, the stem plot would normally be preferable. But since we are very interested in letter grades in this case, perhaps the histogram would be most informative.

1.25 (a) $\bar{x} = 2539 \div 18 = 141.058$. (b) After dropping the outlier, $\bar{x}^* = 2339 \div 17 = 137.588$. This is more in agreement with the "center" found in Exercise 1.9 — the outlier makes the mean higher than it "should" be.

1.26 Since the mean $\bar{x} = \$1.2$ million and number of players on the team is $n + 25$, the team's annual payroll is

$$(\$1.2 \text{ million}) (25) = \$30 \text{ million}$$

If you knew only the median salary, you would not be able to calculate the total payroll because you cannot determine the *sum* of all 25 values from the median. You can only do so when the arithmetic average of the values is provided.

1.27 For Ruth: $M = 46$; for Maris: $M = 24.5$.

1.28 $M = 138.5$. The median is smaller than the mean (141.058), because with the outlier included, the distribution is skewed to the right.

1.29 $\bar{x} = \$480,000 \div 8 = \$60,000$. Seven of the eight employees (everyone but the owner) earned less than the mean. $M = \$22,000$. In recruiting new employees, the owner could correctly say that "the average salary in this company is \$60,000," when it is also true that nobody, except the owner himself, makes that much money.

1.30 The median is the smaller number (\$490,000) — the distribution is skewed to the right, which increases the mean but not the median.

1.31 Yes, the IRQ is a resistant measure of spread. Consider the data set $\{1, 2, 3, 4, 5, 6\}$. The mean and median are both 3.5, $Q_1 = 2$, and $Q_3 = 5$. The IQR is $Q_3 - Q_1 = 5 - 2 = 3$. If the 6 were changed to 100, the IQR would still be $5 - 2 = 3$. The 6 could be any number greater than 5 and the IQR would not change. We conclude that the interquartile range is resistant to extreme observations.

1.32 (a) Ruth: 22 35 46 54 60. Maris: 8 14 24.5 33 61. (b) As in 1.14, we see that for the most part, Ruth had better seasons than Maris.

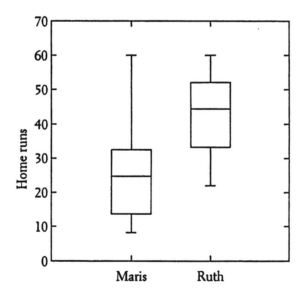

1.33 (a) It appears that M should be about the same as $\bar{x}$, as there is no particular skewness. (b) Five-number summary: 42 51 55 58 69. $\bar{x} = 54.833$, confirming our answer to (a). (c) Between Q_1 and Q_3: 51 to 58.

(d)

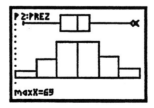

The point 69 is an outlier; this is Ronald Reagan's age on inauguration day. W. H. Harrison was 68, but that is not an outlier according to the 1.5(IQR) test.

1.34 Both boxplots have approximately the same *shape*, although the math scores have a slightly greater range. There is a definite difference in *location*, however: math scores tend to be higher than verbal scores. The *lowest* math score is almost the same as the *median* verbal score.

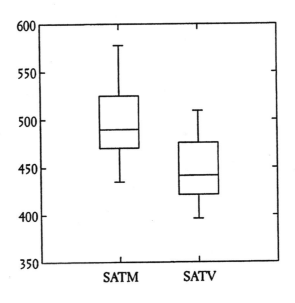

1.35 (a) $\bar{x} = 32.4 \div 6 = 5.4$. (b) $\sum (x_i - \bar{x})^2 = (0.2)^2 + (-0.2)^2 + (-0.8)^2 + (-0.5)^2 + (0.3)^2 + (1.0)^2 = 2.06$; $s^2 = 2.06 \div 5 = 0.412$; $s = \sqrt{0.412} = 0.6419$. (c) [Calculator work.]

1.36 (a) Using $\bar{x} = 41.3$: $\sum (x_i - \bar{x})^2 = 5986.65$; $s^2 = 5986.65 \div 14 = 427.62$; $s = \sqrt{427.62} = 20.68$. (b) Calculators should give $s = 20.61$ (this results from using $\bar{x} = 41\frac{1}{3}$ instead of 41.3). Omitting the two outliers, we find $\bar{x} = 34.54$ and $s = 10.97$ — both quantities had been increased by the skewness.

 If the last observation were changed to 100, the standard deviation s would increase to about 25, so s is not resistant.

1.37 The stemplot reveals two peaks with a "valley" in between — one around 470 and one around 520. The mean and median fall between these two peaks.

```
43 | 7
44 | 013
45 | 9
46 | 113366
47 | 00013368
48 | 144667
49 | 079
50 | 2
51 | 1344799
52 | 1233578
53 | 9
54 | 2368
55 | 5
56 | 4
57 | 7
```

1.38 (a) Stemplot on the next page. (b) $M = 52.3$. (c) $Q_3 = 58.1$; there were landslides in 1964, 1972, and 1984.

```
4 | 33
4 |
5 | 00014
5 | 579
6 | 11
```

1.39 There seems to be little difference between beef and meat hot dogs, but poultry hot dogs are generally lower in calories than the other two. In particular, the median number of calories in a poultry hot dog is smaller than the lower quartiles of the other two, and the poultry lower quartile is less than the minimum calories for beef and meat.

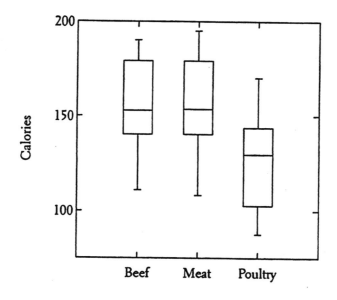

1.40 (a) From the MA and NE regions: 9159, 8500, 6534; and 7914, 5894, 6351, 5504, 6989, 5740. From ESC and SA (excluding DC): 3648, 4390, 3322, 3707; and 6016, 5154, 4860, 6184, 4802, 4327, 5360, 5046. (b) Northeastern: $\bar{x} = 6954$, $s = 1295$; five-number summary: 5504 5817 6534 8207 9159. Southern: $\bar{x} = 4735$, $s = 902$; five-number summary: 3322 3862 4831 5308 6184. (These are Minitab computations; computing by hand gives $Q_1 = 4017$ and $Q_3 = 5257$). The back-to-back stemplot (with southern states on the left and northeastern states on the right) shows the northeastern states are generally well ahead of the southern states in spending per pupil.

```
  763 | 3 |
 9843 | 4 |
  420 | 5 | 579
   20 | 6 | 45
      | 7 | 09
      | 8 | 5
      | 9 | 2
```

1.41 The stemplot on the next page shows the distribution to be fairly symmetrical, with a low outlier of $4.88 - \bar{x}$ and s should be reasonable in this setting. $\bar{x} = 5.4479$ and $s = 0.22095$; the mean $\bar{x}$ serves as our best estimate of the earth's density.

```
48 | 8
49 |
50 | 7
51 | 0
52 | 6799
53 | 04469
54 | 2467
55 | 03578
56 | 12358
57 | 59
58 | 5
```

1.42 Since there are two definite outliers (Alaska and Florida), the five-number summary is preferable; it is 4.2 11.35 12.65 13.7 18.3 (if computed by hand, $Q_1 = 11.4$). For reference, $\bar{x} = 12.544$ and $s = 2.121$.

1.43 The distribution is clearly skewed to the right, with at least the top two salaries (and arguably the top three) as outliers. The five-number summary is appropriate: 109 158 635 2300 6200.

```
0 | 111111111224
0 | 5668
1 | 0
1 | 5
2 | 1133
2 |
3 | 03
3 |
4 | 0
4 |
5 |
5 | 9
6 | 2
```

1.44 The difference in the mean and median indicates that the distribution of awards is skewed sharply to the right—i.e., there are some *very* large awards.

1.45 (a) Mean—although incomes are likely to be right-skewed, the city government wants to know about the total tax base. (b) Median—the sociologist is interested in a "typical" family, and wants to lessen the impact of the extremes.

1.46 The median—half are traveling faster than you, and half are traveling slower. (Actually, you have found *a* median—it could be that a whole range of speeds, say from 56 to 58 mph, might satisfy this condition.)

1.47 (a) 1, 1, 1, 1. (b) 0, 0, 10, 10. (c) For (a), any set of four identical numbers will have $s = 0$. For (b), the answer is unique; here is a rough description of why. We want to maximize the "spread-out"-ness of the numbers (that is what standard deviation measures), so 0 and 10 seem to be reasonable choices based on that idea. We also want to make each individual squared deviation—$(x_1 - \bar{x})^2$, $(x_2 - \bar{x})^2$, $(x_3 - \bar{x})^2$, and $(x_4 - \bar{x})^2$—as large as possible. If we choose 0, 10, 10, 10—or 10, 0, 0, 0—we make the first squared deviation (7.5^2), but the other three are only $(2.5)^2$. Our best choice is two at each extreme, which makes all four squared deviations equal to 5^2.

CHAPTER REVIEW

1.48 (a) Since a person cannot choose the day on which he or she has a heart attack, one would expect that all days are "equally likely" — no day is favored over any other. While there is *some* day-to-day variation, this does seem to be supported by the chart. (b) Monday through Thursday are fairly similar, but there is a pronounced peak on Friday, and lows on Saturday and Sunday. Patients do have some choice about when they leave the hospital, and many probably choose to leave on Friday, perhaps so that they can spend the weekend with the family. Additionally, many hospitals cut back on staffing over the weekend, and they may wish to discharge any patients who are ready to leave before then.

1.49 (a) Stemplot is symmetric with no *obvious* outliers (although 10.17 and 9.75 seem to be unusually high, and 6.75 is extraordinarily low). (b) Plot appears below; note outliers show up more clearly there. (c) $\bar{x} = 8.3628$ and $s = 0.4645$. (d) Between $\bar{x} - s$ and $\bar{x} + s$ (7.8983 to 8.8273): 25 (64.1%). Between $\bar{x} - 2s$ and $\bar{x} + 2s$ (7.4338 to 9.2918): 37 (94.9%). Between $\bar{x} - 3s$ and $\bar{x} + 3s$ (6.9693 to 9.7563): 39 (100%). These compare very nicely with the 68–95–99.7 rule.

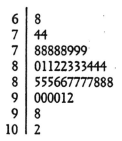

```
 6 | 8
 7 | 44
 7 | 88888999
 8 | 01122333444
 8 | 555667777888
 9 | 000012
 9 | 8
10 | 2
```

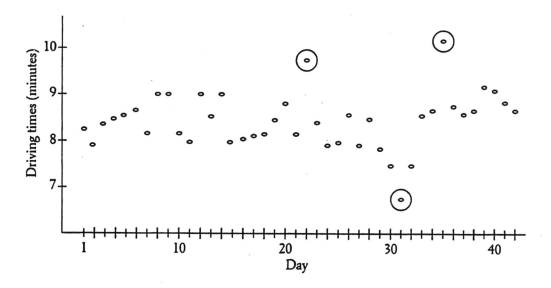

1.50 (a) Normal corn group: 272 333 (or 338) 358 401.2 (or 400.5) 462. New corn group: 318 379.25 (or 383.5) 406.5 429.25 (or 428.5) 477. The boxplot on the next page shows that the new corn seems to increase weight gain — in particular, the median weight gain for new-corn chicks was greater than Q_3 for those that ate normal corn. (b) Normal corn: $\bar{x} = 366.3$, $s = 50.8$; new corn: $\bar{x} = 402.95$, $s = 42.73$. On the average, the chicks that were fed the new corn gained 36.65 grams more mass (weight) than the other chicks.

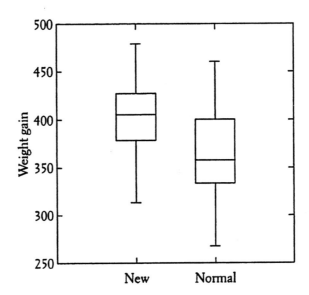

1.51 DiMaggio: 12 20.5 30 32 46. Mantle: 13 21 (or 20.5) 28.5 37 (or 37.75) 54. One might say that DiMaggio seems to have been more consistent — Mantle's plot is more spread out than DiMaggio's. The first three numbers in both summaries are similar, but Mantle's Q_3 and maximum are higher — he apparently had more impressive "big seasons" than DiMaggio.

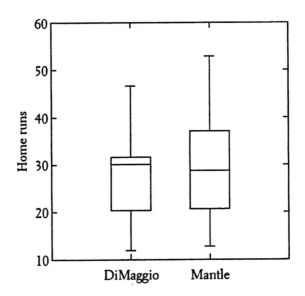

1.52 (a) Stems are split five ways (see next page). Distribution is fairly symmetric, except for the low outlier (15) — taking that into account, this might be considered left-skewed. (b) The Rolls Royce Silver Spur is certainly a gas-guzzler — and possibly the Mercedes S420. (c) 15 24.75 26 28 31 (if done by hand, $Q_1 = 25$). A typical car gets 26 MPG; the top quarter gets at least 28 MPG. (d) $\bar{x} = 25.8$ — slightly lower than the median because of the low outlier (i.e., the left-skewedness).

```
1 | 5
1 |
1 |
2 | 0
2 | 233
2 | 445555
2 | 66666667777
2 | 888999
3 | 11
```

1.53 (a) Stems are the hundreds digit; leaves are tens digit. Clearly skewed to the right (as expected). Main peak occurs from 50 to 150 — the guinea pigs which lived over 500 days are apparent outliers. (b) The mean is larger than the median because it is "drawn out" in the direction of the long tail — to the right. (c) 43 82.25 102.5 153.75 598. The difference between Q_3 and the maximum is relatively much larger than the other differences between successive numbers. This indicates a large "spread" among the high observations — that is, it shows that the data are skewed to the right.

```
0 | 4
0 | 55666677778888888888999999
1 | 00000000000011111222334444
1 | 556678889
2 | 0114
2 | 5
3 | 3
3 | 8
4 | 0
4 |
5 | 12
5 |
6 | 0
```

1.54 (a) Min $= -34.04$, $Q_1 = -2.95$, Med $= 3.47$, $Q_3 = 8.45$, Max $= 58.68$

   (b) 58.68% of $1,000 is $586.80. The stock is worth $1,586.80 at the end of the best month. In the worst month the stock lost 1000 (.3404) = $340.40, so the $1000 decreased in worth to 1000 − 340.40 = $659.60.

   (c) IQR $= Q_3 - Q_1 = 8.45 - (-2.95) = 11.4$
   $1.5 \text{ (IQR)} = 17.1$
   $Q_1 - 17.1 = -2.95 - 17.1 = -20.05$
   $Q_3 + 17.1 = 8.45 = 17.1 = 25.55$
   It appears that SPLUS uses the 1.5 × IQR criterion to identify outliers.

   (d) The distribution is fairly symmetric, with a single peak in the high single digits (5 to 9). There are no gaps, four outliers below, and five outliers above. The mean (3.064) is slightly less than the median (3.4691), suggesting a slight skew to the left.

1.55 (a) After the first two years, the median return is above zero all but once. However, there is no particular evidence of a trend. (b) The spread of the boxplots is considerably smaller in recent years (with the exception of 1987). (c) Four of the five high outliers are visible: 58.7 in 1973, 57.9 in 1975, 32 in 1979, and either 42 or 41.8 in 1974 (the fifth high outlier must have occurred in one of the first three years, so that it was overshadowed by a higher return). The lowest outlier appears in 1973, and the second lowest must have occurred there as well. In 1987, we see a return of either -26.6 or -27. These observations agree with the trend observed in (b) — most of the outliers occurred in the early years, and lately the variability has lessened considerably. The low in 1987 stands out as a "real" deviation from the pattern.

1.56 There is no apparent trend that would support either Julie's or John's position. However, one might observe a trend toward having a greater age spread in recent years (which, if true, is contrary to both positions — we do not simply have many older presidents, or many younger presidents, but rather we have a variety).

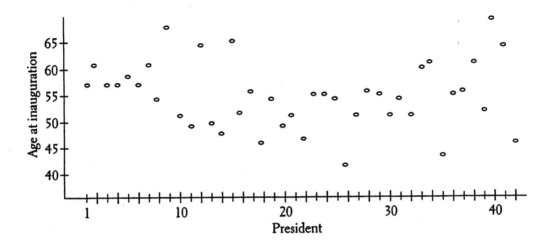

1.57 (a) Below. (b) The plot shows a decreasing trend — fewer disturbances overall in the later years — and more importantly, there is an apparent cyclic behavior. Looking at the table, the spring and summer months (April through September) generally have the most disturbances — probably for the simple reason that more people are outside during those periods.

1.58 These answers will vary with the year. Note that the index of *Statistical Abstract* lists the *table* number, not the *page* number.

1.59 Total value of stock is likely to be skewed to the right — there are a (relatively) few companies with high market values which increase the mean, but not the median. (For example, Microsoft is listed on NASDAQ.)

2

The Normal Distributions

SECTION 2.1

2.1 There are many correct drawings. Here are two possibilities:

(a)   (b)

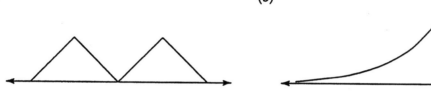

2.2 (a) 20% (the region is a rectangle with height 1 and base width 0.2; hence the area is 0.2). (b) 60%. (c) 50%.

2.3 (a) 0.2 (b) 0.6 (c) 1 (d) 0.35.

2.4 (a) Mean C, median B; (b) mean A, median A; (c) mean A, median B.

2.5 The uniform distribution. Each of the 6 bars should have height of 20.

2.6

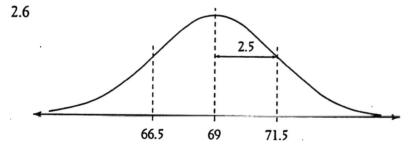

2.7 (a) 2.5% (this is 2 standard deviations above the mean). (b) 69 ± 5; that is, 64 to 74 inches. (c) 16%. (d) 84%. The area to the left of $X = 71.5$ under the $N(69, 2.5)$ curve is 0.84.

2.8 (a) 50%. (b) 2.5%. (c) 110 ± 50, or 60 to 160.

2.9 (a) 50. The mean (center of the distribution in this case) is 64.5, so 50% of the area to the left of 64.5 under the $N(64.5, 2.5)$ curve. Parts (b) through (d) use similar reasoning. (b) 2.5 (c) 84 (d) 99.85.

2.11 Approximately 0.2 (for the tall one) and 0.5.

2.12 (a) 16%. (b) 84th percentile. The area to the left of $X = 23.9$ under the $N(22.8, 1.1)$ curve is 0.84. (c) 68%.

2.13 (a) 266 ± 32, or 234 to 298 days. (b) Less than 234 days. (c) More than 298 days (2 standard deviations to the right of the mean).

2.14 (a) The area to the right of 110 (the mean) under the $N(110, 25)$ curve is 0.5. (b) The area more than 2σ from the mean μ in the right tail is .02275 (approximately half of .05). (c) The area within 2σ of the mean μ is .9545.

2.15 No. Within 4 standard deviations is .999937 area. Going out to 5 standard deviations gives area .999999, which rounds to 1 for 4 decimal place accuracy.

2.16 (a) By the 68-95-99.7 rule, approximately 16% of the scores lie below $\mu - 1\sigma = 110 - 25 = 85$. The TI-83 command shadeNorm $(-1000, 85, 110, 25)$ reports a lower left tail area of .158655. (b) The 84th percentile is the area under the $N(110,25)$ curve to the left of $\mu + 1\sigma = 110 + 25 = 135$. The command shadeNorm $(-1000, 135, 110, 25)$ reports an area of .841345. The 97.5 percentile is the area to the left of $\mu + 2\sigma = 110 + 50 = 160$. ShadeNorm $(-1000, 160, 110, 25)$ reports an area of .97725.

2.17 (a)

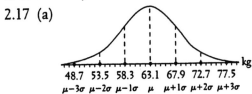

(b) 68%: (58.3, 67.9). 95%: (53.5, 72.7). 99.7%: (48.7, 77.5).

2.18 (a)

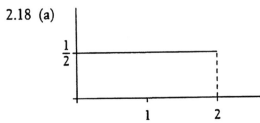

(b) 50% of the outcomes are less than 1. (c) Because the distribution is symmetric, the median is 1, $Q_1 = .5$, and $Q_3 = 1.5$. (d) For $0.5 < X < 1.3$, the proportion of outcomes is 0.8 (1/2) = 0.4.

2.19 (a) Outcomes around 25 are more likely. (d) The distribution should be roughly symmetric with center at about 25, single peaked at the center, standard deviation about 3.5, and few or no outliers. The normal density curve should fit this histogram well.

SECTION 2.2

2.20 Eleanor's z-score is $(680 - 500)/100 = 1.8$; Gerald's is $(27 - 18)/6 = 1.5$. Eleanor's score is higher.

2.21 The standard normal density function is defined by the formula

$$y = \frac{1}{\sigma\sqrt{2\pi}} e^{-\frac{1}{2}\left(\frac{x-\mu}{\sigma}\right)^2}$$

when $\mu = 0$ and $\sigma = 1$.

2.22 (a) 0.9978.

(b) $1 - 0.9978 = 0.0022$.

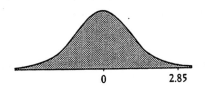

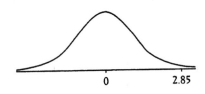

(c) $1 - 0.0485 = 0.9515.$ (d) $0.9978 - 0.0485 = 0.9493.$

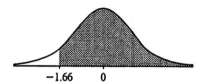

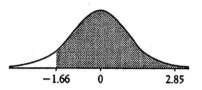

2.23 (a) About -0.675 (-0.67449).   (b) About 0.25 (0.253347).

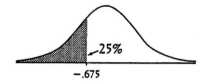

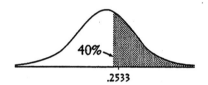

2.24 (a) $z = 3/2.5 = 1.20$; $1 - 0.8849 = 0.1151$; about 11.5%. (b) About 88.5%. (c) 72.2 inches.

2.25 (a) 65.5%. (b) 5.5%. (c) About 127 (or more).

2.26 $\bar{x} = 5.4479$ and $s = 0.22095$. About 75.8% (22 out of 29) lie within one standard deviation of $\bar{x}$, while 96.6% (28/29) lie within two standard deviations.

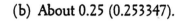

1	2	11	11	4	0
(3.4%)	(6.9%)	(37.9%)	(37.9%)	(13.8%)	(0%)

5.01	5.23	5.45	5.67	5.89
$\bar{x} - 2s$	$\bar{x} - s$	$\bar{x}$	$\bar{x} + s$	$\bar{x} + 2s$

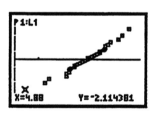

The lineaity of the normal probability plot indicates an approximately normal distribution.

2.27 Cobb: $z = (.420 - .266) \div .0371 = 4.15$; Williams: $z = 4.26$; Brett: $z = 4.07$. Williams z-score is highest.

2.28 (a) 0.0122. (b) 0.9878. (c) 0.0384. (d) 0.9494.

2.29 (a) About 0.84. (b) About 0.385.

2.30 (a) -21.4% to 45%. (b) About 23.9% (23.89%). (c) About 21%.

2.31 (a) About 5.21%. (b) 44%. (c) 279 days or longer.

2.32 (a) At about ± 0.675. (b) For any normal distribution, the quartiles are ± 0.675 standard deviations from the mean; for human pregnancies, the quartiles are 266 ± 10.8, or 255.2 and 276.8.

2.33 (a) At about ± 1.28. (b) 64.5 ± 3.2, or 61.3 to 67.7.

2.34 (a) normalcdf $(-1E99, -2.25) = .0122$ (b) normalcdf $(-2.25, 1E99) = .9878$ (c) normalcdf $(1.77, 1E99) = .0384$ (d) normalcdf $(-2.25, 1.77) = .9494$.

2.36 The mean and standard deviation of a data set of standardized values should be 0 and 1 respectively.

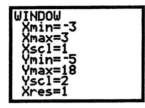   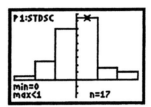

The command 1-Var Stats LSTDSC produces the following screen:

and confirms that the mean is 0 and the standard deviation is 1.

·2.37 The normal probability plot shows a strong linear trend. The presidents' ages are approximately normally distributed.

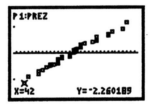

CHAPTER REVIEW

2.38 (a)

Y
$\sqrt{2}$ - - - - - - - - - - • $(\sqrt{2}, \sqrt{2})$

$\sqrt{2}$ X

(b) If X is the coordinate for which the area between 0 and X under the curve is .5, then $1/2 X$ base X height $= X^2/2 = 1/2$. Solving for X: X = 1. The median is 1. The same approach shows that $Q_1 = \sqrt{.5} = .707$ and $Q_3 = \sqrt{1.5} = 1.225$. (c) The mean will lie to the left of the median (1) because the density curve is skewed left. (d) Area $= (.5)(.5)/2 = .125$, so 12.5% of the observations lie below 0.5. None (0%) of the observations lie above 1.5.

2.39 (a)

1.4
1.2
1.0
.8   A | B
.6 •- - - - -|- - - -•
.4
.2   C
0

        .5   1

(b) $M = 0.5, Q_1 = .3, Q_3 = .7$ (c) 25.2% (d) 49.6%

2.40 (a) $X < 20$ corresponds to $Z < (20 - 25)/5 = -1.00$. The relative frequency is .1587. Alternatively, normalcdf $(-1E99, 20, 25, 5) = .1587$. (b) $X < 10$ corresponds to $Z < (10 - 25)/5 = -3.00$. The relative frequency is .0013, normalcdf $(-1E99, 10, 25, 5) = .00135$. (c) The top quarter corresponds to $z = .675$. Solving $.675 = (x - 25)/5$ gives 28.38.

2.41 13.

2.42 The proportion scoring below 1.7 is about 0.052; the proportion between 1.7 and 2.1 is about 0.078.

2.43 Soldiers whose head circumference is outside the range 22.8 ± 1.81, approximately, less than 21 inches or greater than 24.6 inches.

2.44 Those scoring at least 3.42 are in the "most Anglo/English" 30%; those scoring less than 2.58 make up the "most Mexican/Spanish" 30%.

2.45 (a) Using the window dimensions shown, the histogram shows a distribution that is fairly symmetric with no obvious outliers (a boxplot shows that 10.17 is an outlier). The mean (8.40) is approximately equal to the median (8.42), an indication of symmetry.

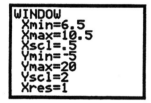
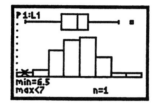
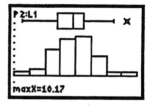

(b) We remove 6.75 (the day after Thanksgiving), and the two largest times, 9.75 and 10.17 (icy roads and a delay due to a traffic accident). The remaining data are slightly skewed left; the mean (8.36) is less than the median (8.42).

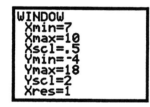
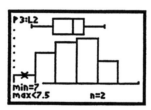
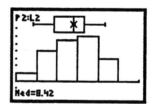

2.46 The normal probability plot for the weight gain for the chicks in the control group (normal corn) is:

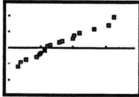

where the observed weight gain is on the x-axis and the standardized value is on the y-axis. The normal probability plot for the experimental group of chicks fed the lysine added diet is:

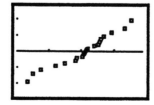

Both plots show a fairly linear pattern of points, so we conclude that both distributions are approximately normal. Thus it is reasonable to use x and s for the center and spread of the distributions.

3

Examining Relationships

INTRODUCTION

3.1 Height at age six is explanatory, and height at age 16 is the response variable. Both are quantitative.

3.2 Sex is explanatory, and political preference in the last election is the response. Both are categorical.

3.3 "Treatment" — old or new — is the (categorical) explanatory variable. Survival time is the (quantitative) response variable.

3.4 The variables are: SAT math score; SAT verbal score. There is no explanatory/response relationship. Both variables are quantitative.

SECTION 3.1

3.5 (a) Explanatory variable: jet skis in use.

(b)

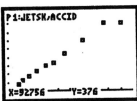

The horizontal axis is "Jet Skis in Use," and the vertical axis is "Accidents." There is a strong explanatory-response relationship between the number of jet skis in use (explanatory) and the number of accidents (response).

3.6 Answers will vary.

3.7 (a) The variables are positively associated, that is, as the number of jet skis in use increases, the number of accidents also increases. (b) The association is linear. (c) The association appears to be strong. By taking two representative points and finding the equation of the straight line that passes through those two points, we obtain the approximate equation $y = .005x$. When $x = 1,000,000$ jet skis in use, $y = 5,000$ accidents.

3.8 (a) Plot is on page 23; speed is explanatory. (b) The relationship is curved — low in the middle, higher at the extremes. Since low "mileage" is actually *good* (it means that we use less fuel to travel 100 km), this makes sense: moderate speeds yield the best performance. Note that 60 km/hr is about 37 mph. (c) Above-average values of "mileage" are found with both low and high values of "speed." (d) The relationship is very strong — there is little scatter around the curve, and it is very useful for prediction.

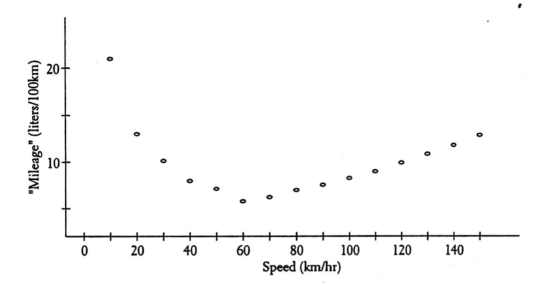

3.9 (a) See plot below. Body mass is the explanatory variable. (b) Positive association, linear, moderately strong. (c) The male subjects' plot can be described in much the same way, though the scatter appears to be greater. The males typically have larger values for both variables.

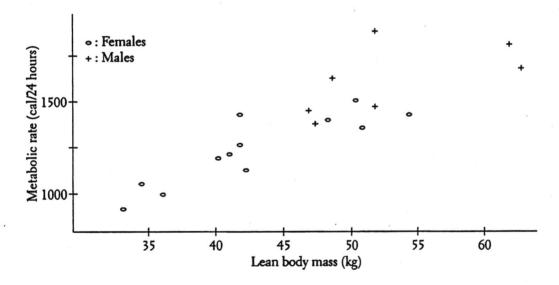

3.10 (a) Two mothers are 57 inches tall; their husbands are 66 and 67 inches tall. (b) The tallest fathers are 74 inches tall; there are three of them, and their wives are 62, 64, and 67 inches tall. (c) There is no clear explanatory variable; either could go on the horizontal axis. (d) The weak positive association indicates that people have *some* tendency to marry persons of a similar *relative* height — but it is not an overwhelming tendency. It is weak because there is a great deal of scatter.

3.11 (a) Lowest: about 107 calories (with about 145 mg of sodium); highest: about 195 calories, with about 510 mg of sodium. (b) There is a positive association; high-calorie hot dogs tend to be high in salt, and low-calorie hot dogs tend to have low sodium. (c) The lower left point is an outlier. Ignoring this point, the remaining points seem to fall roughly on a line. The relationship is moderately strong.

3.12 (a) See plot on page 24. (b) Positive association; approximately linear save for two outliers (circled): spaghetti and the snack cake.

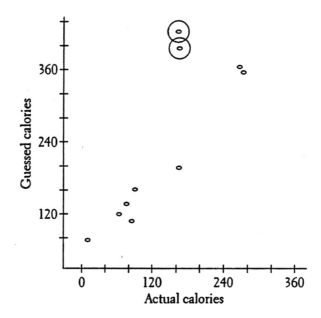

3.13 Since there is no obvious choice for response variable, either could go on the vertical axis. The plot shows a strong positive linear relationship, with no outliers. There appears to be only one species represented.

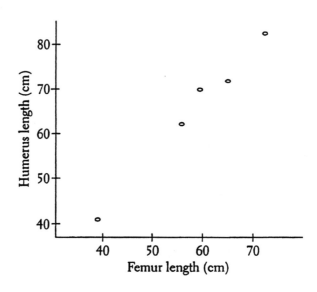

3.14

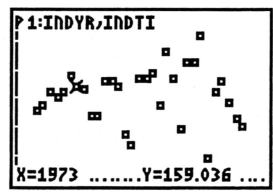

The point (1973, 159.036) appears to fit the trend up to that time, but the points (1975, 149.213) and (1976, 148.725) both show dramatic drops in average speed. The explanation may be that mandatory caution flags, waved before the race was stopped, caused average speeds to drop.

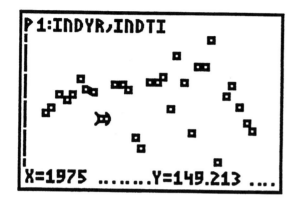
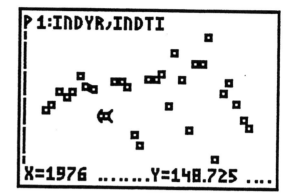

3.15 (a) Planting rate is explanatory. (b) See (d). (c) As we might expect from the discussion, the pattern is curved — high in the middle, and lower on the ends. Not linear, and there is neither positive nor negative association. (d) 20,000 plants per acre seems to give the highest average yield.

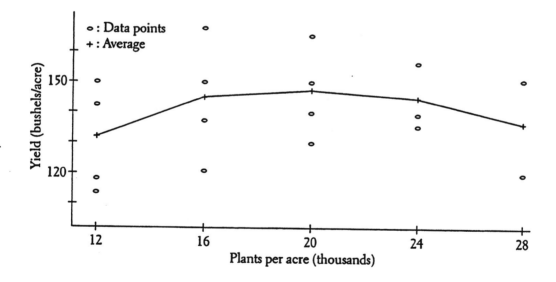

3.16 (a) There should be a positive association because money spent for teacher salaries is part of the education budget; more money spent per pupil would typically translate to more money spent overall. (b) See (e). (c) The plot on page 26 shows a positive, approximately linear relationship. (d) California, spending $4,826 per pupil, with median teacher salary $39,600. (e) The mountain states are clustered down in the lower left: They spend lower-than-average amounts per student, and have low median teacher salaries.

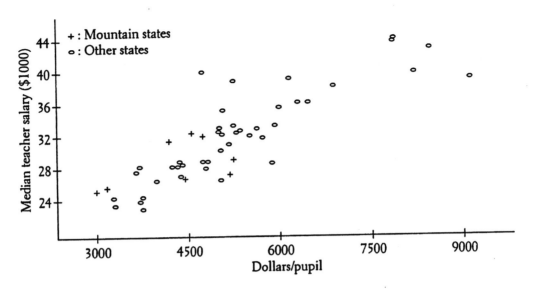

3.17 (a) Plot is below. The means are (in the order given) 47.167, 15.667, 31.5, and 14.833. (b) Yellow seems to be the most attractive, and green is second. White and blue are poor attractors. (c) Positive or negative association make no sense here because color is a categorical variable (what is an "above-average" color?).

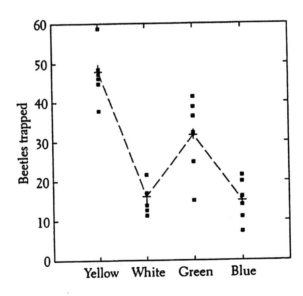

SECTION 3.2

3.18 (a)

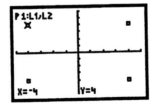

There appears to be no association between x and y. The mean and standard deviation for both x and y are 0 and 4.62, respectively.

x	y	$\dfrac{x-\bar{x}}{s_x}$	$\dfrac{y-\bar{y}}{s_y}$	$\left(\dfrac{x-\bar{x}}{s_x}\right)\left(\dfrac{y-\bar{y}}{s_y}\right)$
4	-4	.866	$-.866$	$-.75$
4	4	.866	.866	.75
-4	4	$-.866$	.866	$-.75$
-4	-4	$-.866$	$-.866$	.75
			TOTAL	0

$$r = \frac{1}{n-1}\sum\left(\frac{x-\bar{x}}{s_x} \times \frac{y-\bar{y}}{s_y}\right) = 0$$

(b)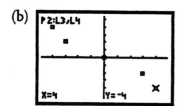

$$\bar{x} = 0,\ s_x = 3.5355,\ y = 0,\ s_y = 3.1623$$

x	y	$\dfrac{x-\bar{x}}{s_x}$	$\dfrac{y-\bar{y}}{s_y}$	$\left(\dfrac{x-\bar{x}}{s_x}\right)\left(\dfrac{y-\bar{y}}{s_y}\right)$
4	-4	1.1314	-1.2649	-1.43
3	-2	.8485	$-.6325$	$-.5367$
0	0	0	0	0
-3	2	$-.8485$	.6325	$-.5367$
-4	4	-1.1314	1.2649	-1.431
			TOTAL	-3.9355

$$r = \frac{-3.9355}{4} = -.98$$

(c)

$$\bar{x} = 0,\ s_x = 3.65,\ \bar{y} = 0,\ s_y = 3.65$$

x	y	$\dfrac{x-x}{s_x}$	$\dfrac{y-y}{s_y}$	$\left(\dfrac{x-x}{s_x}\right)\left(\dfrac{y-y}{s_y}\right)$
4	4	1.0954	1.0954	1.2
2	-2	.5477	$-.5477$	$-.3$
-2	2	$-.5477$	.5477	$-.3$
-4	-4	-1.0954	-1.0954	1.2
			TOTAL	1.8

$$r = \frac{1}{n-1}(1.8) = \frac{1.8}{3} = 0.6$$

The association is positive, but it is not strong.

3.19 (a) With x as femur length and y as humerus length: $\bar{x} = 58.2$, $s_x = 13.20$; $\bar{y} = 66.0$, $s_y = 15.89$; $r = 0.994$.

3.20 Because there is no obvious linear relationship, one expects the correlation to be near zero.

3.21 Clearly positive (there is positive association), but not near 1 (there is a fair amount of scatter).

3.22 $r = 1$.

3.23 (a) See Exercise 3.13 for plot. The plot shows a strong positive linear relationship, with little scatter, so we expect that r is close to 1. (b) r would not change — it is computed from standardized values, which have no units.

3.24 With x for speed and y for mileage: $\bar{x} = 40$, $s_x = 15.8$; $\bar{y} = 26.8$, $s_y = 2.68$; $r = 0$. Correlation only measures *linear* relationships; this plot shows a strong *non-linear* relationship.

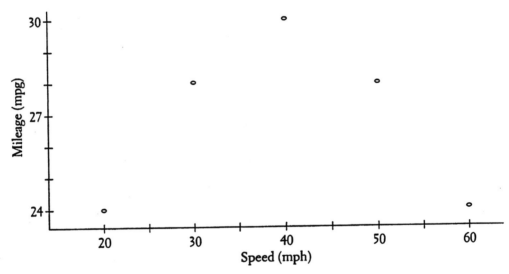

3.25 (a) See Exercise 3.9 for plot. Both correlations should be positive, but since the men's data seem to be more spread out, it may be slightly smaller. (b) Women: $r_w = 0.87645$; Men: $r_m = 0.59207$. (c) Women: $\bar{x}_w = 43.03$; Men: $\bar{x}_m = 53.10$. The difference in means has no effect on the correlation. (d) There would be no change, since standardized measurements are dimensionless.

3.26 (a) See Exercise 3.12 for plot. $r = 0.82450$. This agrees with the positive association observed in the plot; it is not too close to 1 because of the outliers. (b) It has no effect on the correlation. If every guess had been 100 calories higher — or 1000, or 1 million — the correlation would have been exactly the same, since the standardized values would be unchanged. (c) The revised correlation is $r = 0.98374$. The correlation got closer to 1 because without the outliers, the relationship is much stronger.

3.27 (a) Here is the scatterplot of the original x-y data (marked with □).

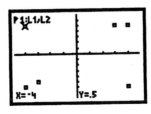

(b) Here is the scatterplot of the transformed data (marked with +), plotted with the original *x-y* data.

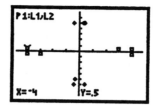

(c) The correlation of the original *x-y* data is 0.253.

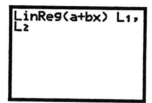
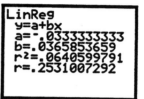

The correlation of the transformed data is also 0.253.

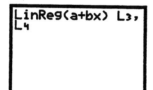
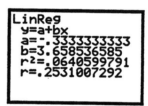

For the first set of data, the *x* values range from −4 to 4, a spread of 8 units, while the spread in the *y* direction is only 1.1 units. For the second data set, the horizontal spread is small (only 0.8 units) compared to the vertical spread of 11 units. What matters in computing the correlation is not the actual sizes of the spreads in each direction (which is what we perceive in this plot), but rather the relative sizes of these spreads, which is more difficult to see unless we make two separate plots, each with appropriate *x* and *y* scales. Here is a different look at the transformed data, this time with different *x* and *y* scales. Notice how much it now looks like the plot (P1) of the original data.

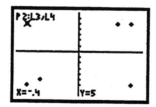

3.28 The person who wrote the article interpreted a correlation close to 0 as if it were a correlation close to −1. Prof. McDaniel's findings mean there is little linear association between research and teaching — for example, knowing a professor is a good researcher gives little information about whether she is a good or bad teacher.

3.29 The plot is given in problem 3.8. $r = -0.17162$ — it is close to zero because the relationship is a curve rather than a line.

3.30 (a) Sex is a categorical variable. (b) r must be between −1 and 1. (c) r should have no units (i.e., it can't be 0.23 *bushel*).

SECTION 3.3

3.31 $\bar{x} = 22.31$, $s_x = 17.74$; $\bar{y} = 5.306$, $s_y = 3.368$; $r = 0.99526$. Except for roundoff error, we again find $b = 0.1890$ and $a = 1.0892$.

3.32 Answers will vary.

3.33 (a) A negative association — the pH decreased (i.e., the acidity increased) over the 150 weeks. (b) The initial pH was 5.4247; the final pH was 4.6350. (c) The slope is -0.0053; the pH decreased by 0.0053 units per week (on the average).

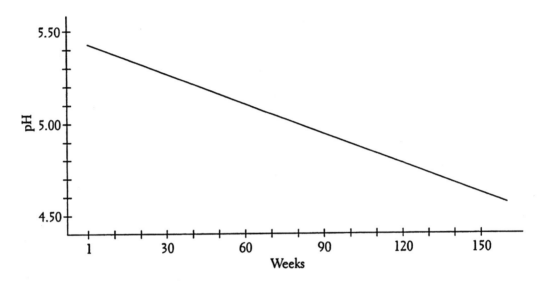

3.34 (a) Below. (b) The slope is close to 1 — meaning that the strength after 28 days is *approximately* (strength after one week) plus 1389 psi. In other words, we expect the extra three weeks to add about 1400 psi of strength to the concrete. (c) 4557 psi.

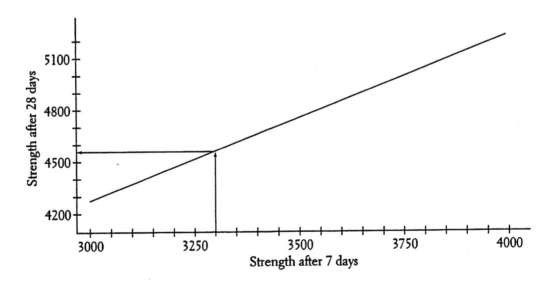

3.35 The LSRL passes through $(\bar{x}, \bar{y})$ if the coordinates satisfy the equation of the regression line (i.e., makes it a true statement). We are given that the y-intercept for the regression line is $a = \bar{y} - b\bar{x}$. Then $\bar{y} = a + b\bar{x}$, so the point $(\bar{x}, \bar{y})$ satisfies the equation.

3.36 (a) $b = r \times s_y \div s_x = 0.16$; $a = \bar{y} - b\bar{x} = 30.2$. (b) $\hat{y} = 78.2$ (c) $r^2 = 0.36$; only 36% of the variability in y is accounted for by the regression, so the estimate $\hat{y} = 78.2$ could be quite different from the real score.

3.37 (a) Below. (b) There is a very strong positive linear relationship; $r = 0.9990$. (c) Regression line: $\hat{y} = 1.76608 + 0.080284x$ (y is steps/second, x is speed). (d) $r^2 = 0.998$, so nearly all the variation (99.8% of it) in steps taken per second is explained by the linear relationship. (e) The regression line would be different (as in Example 3.11), because the line in (c) is based on minimizing the sum of the squared *vertical* distances on the graph. This new regression would minimize the squared *horizontal* distances (for the graph shown). r^2 would remain the same, however.

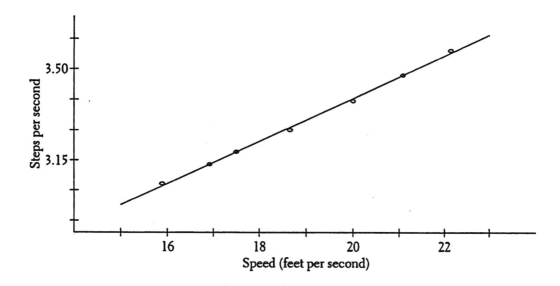

3.38 $r = \sqrt{0.16} = 0.40$ (high attendance goes with high grades, so the correlation must be positive).

3.39 (a) Below. (b) The line is clearly *not* a good predictor of the actual data — it is too high in the middle and too low on each end. (c) The sum is -0.01 — a reasonable discrepancy allowing for round-off error. (d) A straight line is not the appropriate model for these data.

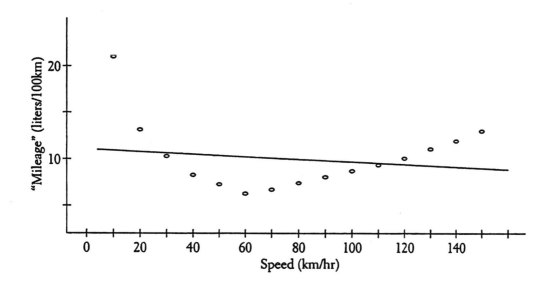

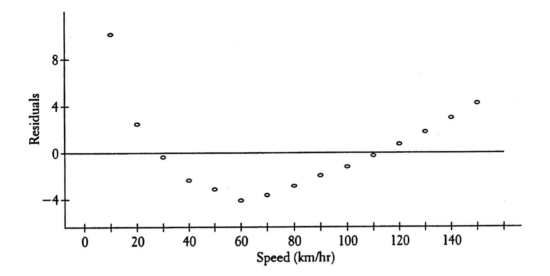

3.40 (a) Below. (b) Let y be "guessed calories" and x be actual calories. Using all points: $\hat{y} = 58.59 + 1.3036x$ (and $r^2 = 0.68$) — the dashed line. Excluding spaghetti and snack cake: $\hat{y}^* = 43.88 + 1.14721x$ (and $r^2 = 0.968$). (c) The two removed points could be called influential, in that when they are included, the regression line passes above every *other* point; after removing them, the new regression line passes through the "middle" of the remaining points.

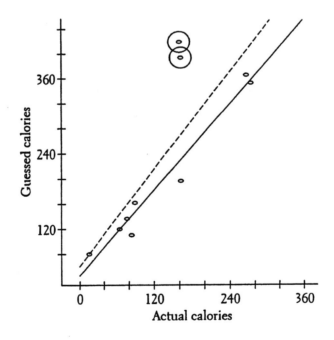

3.41 (a) Without Child 19, $\hat{y}^* = 109.305 - 1.1933x$. Child 19 might be considered *somewhat* influential, but removing this data point does not change the line substantially. (b) With all children, $r^2 = 0.410$; without Child 19, $r^2 = 0.572$. With Child 19's high Gesell score removed, there is less scatter around the regression line — more of the variation is explained by the regression.

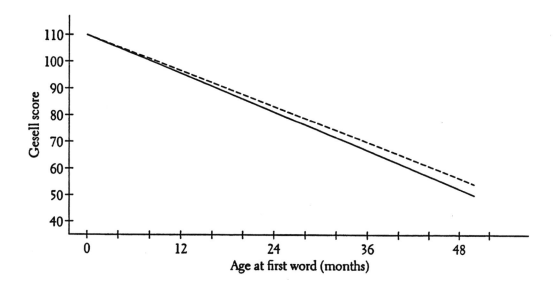

3.42 (a) Graph not shown. (b) $2,500. (c) $y = 500 + 200x$.

3.43 (a) y (weight) $= 100 + 40x$ grams. (b) Graph not shown. (c) When $x = 104$, $y = 4260$ grams, or about 9.4 pounds — a rather frightening prospect. The regression line is only reliable for "young" rats; like humans, rats do not grow at a constant rate throughout their entire life.

3.44 Approximately 650 km/sec. Since there is quite a bit of variation around the line, and $r^2 = 0.615$, we should not have *too* much faith in the accuracy of this estimate.

3.45 (a) Below. (b) $\hat{y} = 71.950 + 0.38333x$. (c) When $x = 40$, $\hat{y} = 87.2832$; when $x = 60$, $\hat{y} = 94.9498$. (d) Sarah is growing at about 0.38 cm/month; she should be growing about 0.5 cm each month $(0.5 = \frac{6}{60-48})$.

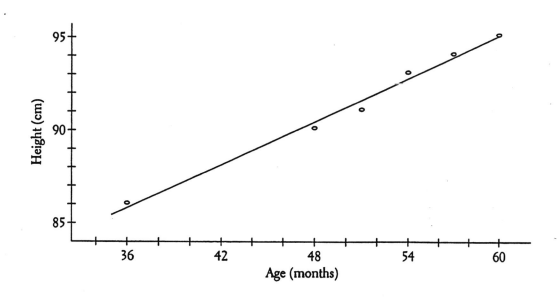

3.46 (a) See plot below. (b) $r = 0.5215$, and $r^2 = 0.2720$. There is a moderate positive association between U.S. and overseas stock returns; this relationship allows us to explain about 27% of the variation in one quantity with the other. (c) The regression line is $\hat{y} = 5.9546 + .7136x$. (d) $\hat{y} = 22.4\%$. We can only explain about one-third of the variation in overseas returns with the U.S. return information, as evidenced by the wide scatter around the line, so we should not expect too much accuracy in our predictions. (e) The outlier point occurred in 1986. The two points on the left end of the graph — from 1973 and 1974 — are potentially influential, especially the far left point.

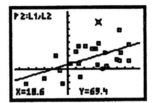

3.47 When $x = 480$, $\hat{y} = 255.95$ cm, or 100.77 in, or about 8.4 feet!

3.48 (a) U.S. stocks: -26.4 3.2 16.8 27 37.6 Overseas stocks: -23.2 .3 12.8 31.1 69.4. (b) Overseas stocks generally had higher returns — as the five-number summaries and the boxplots show, a quarter of the time they did better than 30%. (c) The overseas stocks also fluctuated much more wildly — $(Q_3 - Q_1)$ is about 30% larger for overseas stocks, and the boxplot shows a lot more spread.

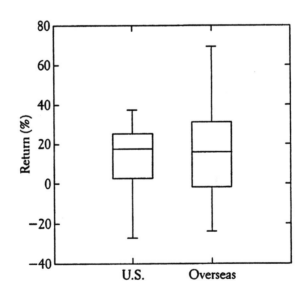

3.49 (a) About 69.4% of the variation is explained ($r^2 = 0.694$). (b) The sum is zero. (c) The residuals change from negative to positive in 1991 — the year the change was made. In that year, the regression line changes from overestimating to underestimating.

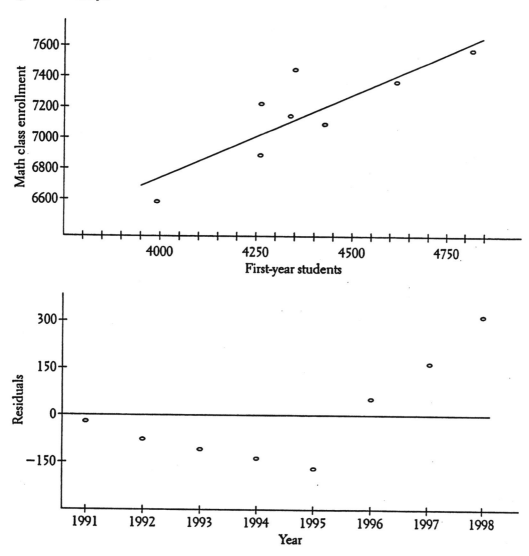

CHAPTER REVIEW

3.50 (a) Powerboat registrations.

(b)

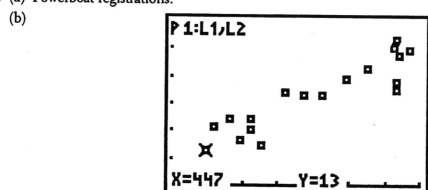

(c) Yes, it appears that there is a strong straight-line pattern. The value of r^2 is 0.833, so 83.3% of the variation in manatees killed is explained by least-squares regression of powerboat registrations on manatees killed.

3.51

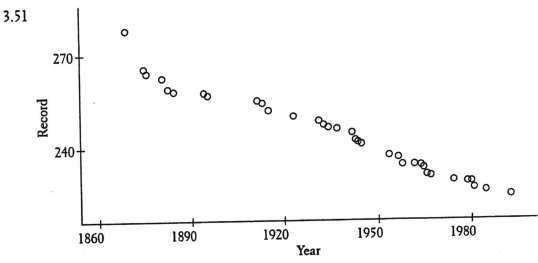

The variables are negatively associated; there is a downward trend. The mile record is decreasing over time. Here is a partial Minitab output:

```
Correlation of Year and Record = −0.983
The regression equation is     Record = 950 − 0.364 Year
```

Unusual Observations

Obs.	Year	Record	Fit	Stdev.Fit	Residual	St.Resid
1	1868	278.800	269.266	0.920	9.534	4.03R
6	1884	258.400	263.436	0.756	−5.036	−2.08R

R denotes an obs. with a large st. resid.

Here is the scatterplot with the regression line:

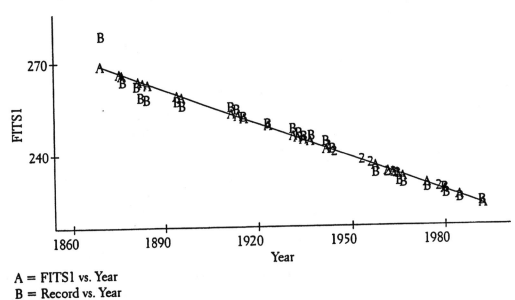

A = FITS1 vs. Year
B = Record vs. Year

The regression line appears to be an excellent model for the data. The correlation is −0.983, and this indicates a strong negative association. Minitab identifies two regression outliers: a high outlier in 1868 and a low outlier in 1884. There appear to be no influential observations. On average, approximately $(226.3-266.0)/(1985-1874) = -.358$ or a little more than a third of a second was lopped off the record each year. It should be safe to predict the world record in 2000, but it may be risky to predict the record in 2005.

3.52 (a) 6. (b) 2. (c) 5. (d) 8. (e) 3. (f) 7. (g) 4. (h) 1.

If you want to duplicate these scatterplots, here are the data. Notice that in the first group of four data sets, the first 8 points are always the same. Then we look at the effect of a ninth point. The same is true for the second group of four data sets.

x1	y1	x2	y2	x3	y3	x4	y4
2	2	2	2	2	2	2	2
3	1	3	1	3	1	3	1
4	2	4	2	4	2	4	2
5	3	5	3	5	3	5	3
5	4	5	4	5	4	5	4
6	4	6	4	6	4	6	4
7	3	7	3	7	3	7	3
8	5	8	5	8	5	8	5
		5	10	15	6	15	1

x5	y5	x6	y6	x7	y7	x8	y8
1	5	1	5	1	5	1	5
2	3	2	3	2	3	2	3
3	4	3	4	3	4	3	4
4	4	4	4	4	4	4	4
4	3	4	3	4	3	4	3
5	2	5	2	5	2	5	2
6	1	6	1	6	1	6	1
7	2	7	2	7	2	7	2
		15	7	12	3	1	10

3.53 (a) Start with points (1, 1) and (2, 2). Then add the influential point (0, 4).

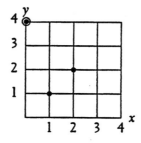

(b) Start with the set of points (1, 1), (1, 2), (2, 1.1), and (2, 2). Then add the influential point (10, 10).

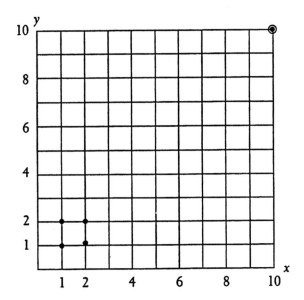

3.54 The TI-83 reports that the correlation $r = .0005$ and $r^2 = 3 \times 10^{-7}$. The points generally show no association. The regression line is not useful as a way to predict average speed.

```
LinReg
 y=a+bx
 a=155.2373137
 b=5.5685484E-4
 r²=2.966787E-7
 r=5.4468224E-4
```

For comparison, here is a partial Minitab output:

```
The regression equation is
AveSpeed = 155 + 0.001 Year
```

Predictor	Coef	Stdev	t-ratio	p
Constant	155.3	376.3	0.41	0.683
Year	0.0005	0.1898	0.00	0.998

```
s = 9.454      R-sq = 0.0%      R-sq(adj) = 0.0%
```

Unusual Observations

Obs.	Year	AveSpeed	Fit	Stdev.Fit	Residual	St.Resid
25	1991	176.46	156.35	2.41	20.11	2.20R
26	1992	134.48	156.35	2.55	−21.87	−2.40R

```
R denotes an obs. with a large st. resid.
```

Minitab finds two data points whose standardized residuals are larger (in absolute value) than 2, and calls these regression outliers. It does not find any influential observations.

There has been more variation in speeds in recent years. It would seem that with more powerful and efficient engines and generally better technology, average speeds would gradually increase, and one can see a subset of the points that describes such an association. But accidents and caution flags lower average speeds, and these can't be predicted.

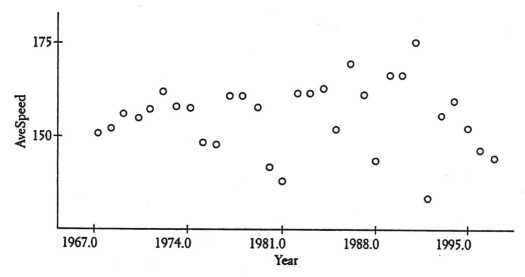

And here is an interesting fact about the Indianapolis average speed data. Because the regression line is so close to horizontal (slope = .0005), the residual plot looks almost identical to the original scatterplot with the regression line.

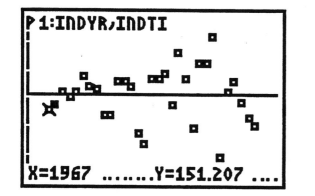

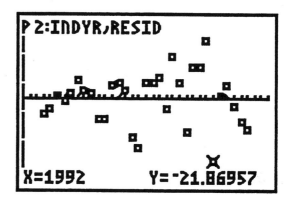

3.55 (a) Franklin is marked with a + (in the lower left corner). (b) There is a moderately strong positive linear association. (It turns out that r^2 = 87.0%.) There are no really extreme observations, though Bank 9 did rather well. Franklin does not look out of place. (c) $\hat{y} = 7.573 + 4.9872x$. (d) Franklin's predicted income was $\hat{y}$ = 26.5 million dollars — almost twice the actual income. The residual is -12.7.

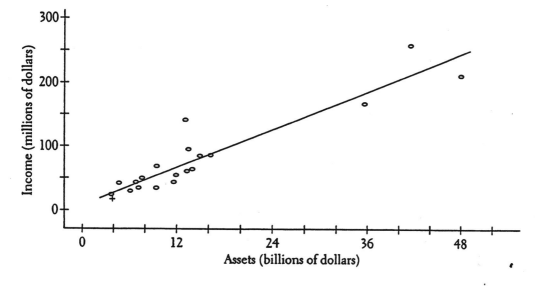

3.56 (a) The men's times (the plot of L_2 on L_1) have been steadily decreasing for the last 100 years.

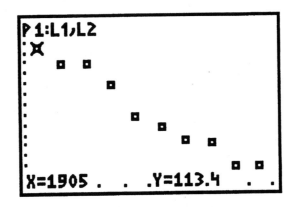

Likewise, the women's times (in the plot of L_4 on L_3) have also been decreasing steadily.

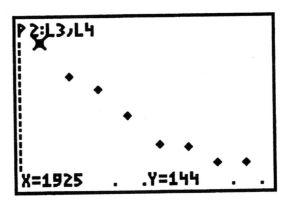

A straight line appears to be a reasonable model for the men's times; the correlation for the men is $r = .983$.

 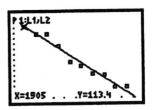

A straight line also appears to be a reasonable model for the women's times; the correlation for the women is $r = -.9687$.

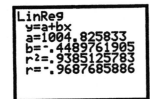 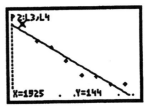

In order to plot both scatterplots on the same axes, we deleted the first two men's times (1905 and 1915). The resulting plot suggests that while the women's scores were decreasing faster than the men's times from 1925 through 1965, the times for both sexes from 1975 have tended to flatten out. In fact, for the period 1925 to 1995, the best model may not be a straight line, but rather a curve, such as an exponential function. In any event, it is not clear, as Whitt and Ward suggest, that women will soon outrun men.

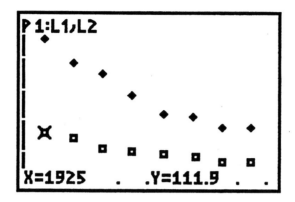

To find out where the two regression lines intersect, set the Window as shown and plot the two lines together. Selecting 2nd / CALC / 5:Intersect yields the point (2002.09, 96.956).

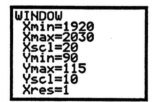 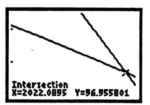

3.57 The plot shows an apparent negative association between nematode count and seedling growth. The correlation supports this: $r = -0.78067$. This also indicates that about 61% of the variation in growth can be accounted for by a linear relationship with nematode count.

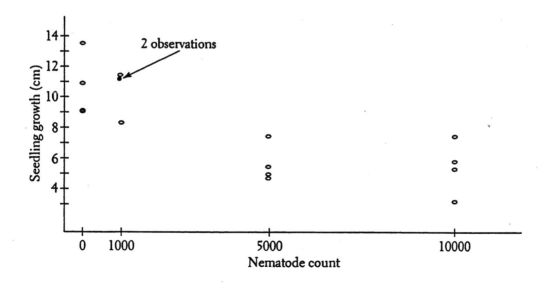

3.58 $b = 0.54$ (and $a = 33.67$). For $x = 67$ inches, we estimate $\hat{y} = 69.85$ inches.

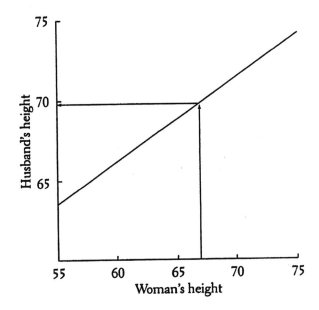

3.59 (a) No. See Exercise 3.53. (b) No. See Exercise 3.53.

3.60 Minimizing the sum of the perpendicular distances from the points to the line would seem like a good idea, but it would be much more complicated algebraically. Another possibility would be to minimize the sum of the horizontal deviations. But this would not be very helpful, because we want to use the resulting straight line to help us predict values of y, given values of x, not the other way around.

4

More on Two-Variable Data

SECTION 4.1

4.1 (a)

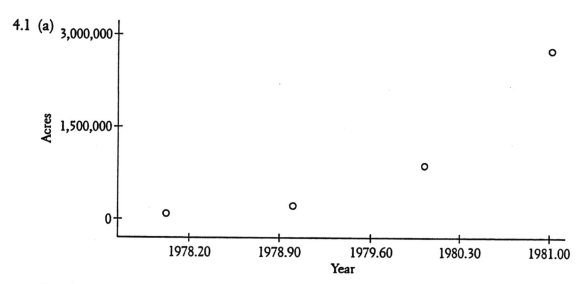

(b) The ratios are 226,260/63,042 = 3.59, 907,075/226,260 = 4.01, and 2,826,095/907,075 = 3.12.

(c) log y yields 4.7996, 5.3546, 5.9576, and 6.4512. Here is the plot of log y vs. x.

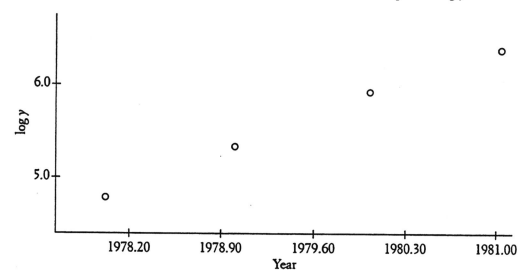

(d) Defining list L_3 on the TI-83 to be $\log(L_2)$ and then performing linear regression on (L_1, L_3) where L_1 holds the year (x) and L_3 holds the log acreage yield the least squares line $\log \hat{y} = -1094.507 + .55577x$. For comparison, Minitab reports

```
The regression equation is
 log y = - 1095 + 0.556 Year
```

Predictor	Coef	Stdev	t-ratio	p
Constant	−1094.51	29.26	−37.41	0.001
Year	0.55577	0.01478	37.60	0.001

s = 0.03305   R−sq = 99.9%   R−sq(adj) = 99.8%

(e)

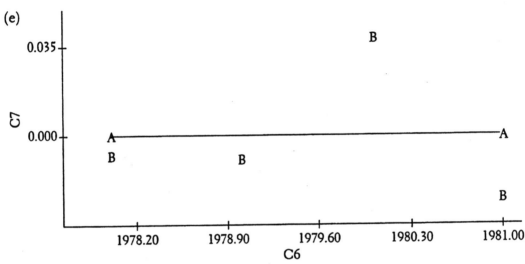

A = C7 vs. C6
B = RESI2 vs. Year

The residual plot of the transformed data shows no clear pattern, so the line is a reasonable model for these points.

(f) $\log \hat{y} = -1094.51 + .5558x$, so $10^{-\log \hat{y}} = 10^{(-1694.51 + .5558x)}$, and so $\hat{y} = 10^{(-1094.51 + .5558x)}$. With the regression equation for $\log y$ on x installed as Y_1 on the TI-83, define $Y_2 = 10 \wedge (Y_1)$. Then plot the original scatterplot and Y_2 together.

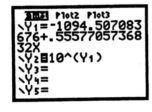
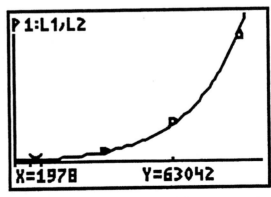

(g) The predicted number of acres defoliated in 1982 is the exponential function evaluated at 1982, which gives 10,719,964.92 acres.

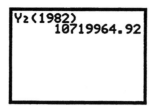

4.2 (a) The scatterplot of the public debt (in trillions) versus coded year (x = number of years since 1980).

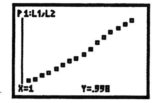

(b) The ratios of consecutive y values are: 1.144, 1.206, 1.142, 1.160, 1.166, 1.107, 1.098, 1.132, 1.091, 1.085, 1.064, 1.060. The mean ratio is 1.12. (c) Install the coded year (x) in list L_1, and the public debt in trillions (y) in L_2. Then define $L_3 = \log(L_2)$.

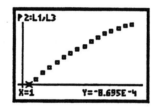

(d) Here is a scatterplot of log (debt) vs. coded year for the last 10 years:

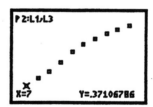

(e) Performing regression on this reduced data set, we obtain

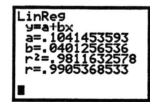 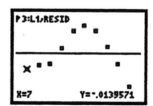

The correlation is $r = .99$ indicating a very strong positive association. The residual plot shows some problems with the linear model: there is a clearly curve pattern to the points. We conclude that the straight line is not the best model.

(f) Performing the inverse transformation, we obtain

$$\log \hat{y} = .1041 + .0401x$$

$$10^{\log \hat{y}} = \hat{y} = 10^{(.1041 + .0401x)}$$

Here is the original scatterplot of the last 10 years with the exponential function.

 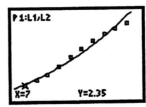

(g) Concerted efforts by President Clinton and Congress to achieve a balanced budget, combined with an unusual period of several years of robust economy in the mid 1990s, slowed the growth of the public debt. The U.S. economy was so strong that the country actually achieved a budget surplus in 1998. The exponential model predicts the public debt in 1977 to be $6,113,381,118,000 (6.113 trillion). The actual debt in 1997 was 5.413 trillion. Note that the public debt was still growing, but the rate of growth was not as great as our model predicts.

(h) The residual plot that stops in 1996 suggests that our model will not be a very good predictor in the future, such as in the year 2000.

4.3 (a) On the TI-83: With the lengths of the fish in list LEN and the weights in list WT, logs of the lengths in list LOGL and the logs of the weights in list LOGW, and the power equation installed as Y_2, define list L_1 to be Y_2(LEN). These are the predicted weights of the fish. Then define list L_2 to be the observed weights minus the predicted weights: WT-L_1. Then use the command STAT / 1-Var Stats L_2.
The sum of the squares of the deviations, $\Sigma x^2 = 7795.687$. Here are the lists:

Age	Len (cm)	Wt (g)	log (Len)	log (Wt)	Predict	Deviatns
1	5.2	2	0.71600	0.30103	1.923	0.0770
2	8.5	8	0.92942	0.90309	8.605	−0.6054
3	11.5	21	1.06070	1.32222	21.632	−0.6319
4	14.3	38	1.15534	1.57978	42.042	−4.0421
5	16.8	69	1.22531	1.83885	68.716	0.2835
6	19.2	117	1.28330	2.06819	103.253	13.7472
7	21.3	148	1.32838	2.17026	141.698	6.3020
8	23.3	190	1.36736	2.27875	186.302	3.6978
9	25.0	264	1.39794	2.42160	230.930	33.0696
10	26.7	293	1.42651	2.46687	282.232	10.7679
11	28.2	318	1.45025	2.50243	333.421	−15.4207
12	29.6	371	1.47129	2.56937	386.509	−15.5092
13	30.8	455	1.48855	2.65801	436.304	18.6958
14	32.0	504	1.50515	2.70243	490.238	13.7617
15	33.0	518	1.51851	2.71433	538.467	−20.4672
16	34.0	537	1.53148	2.72997	589.786	−52.7863
17	34.9	651	1.54283	2.81358	638.697	12.3032
18	36.4	719	1.56110	2.85673	726.149	−7.1486
19	37.1	726	1.56937	2.86094	769.576	−43.5762
20	37.7	810	1.57634	2.90848	808.162	1.8384

The quantity that was *minimized* was the sum of the squares of the deviations of the transformed points.
(b) Note that you can't use 1-Var Stats to find the sum of the squares of the residuals in the list RESID; you need to first copy the list RESID into a different list. The sum of the squares of the residuals is .0143.
(c) There's no reason to expect the answers to be the same.

4.4 (a) As height increases, weight increases. Since weight is a 3-dimensional attribute and height is 1-dimensional, weight should be proportional to the cube of the height. One might speculate a model of the form WEIGHT = a × HEIGHT$^{\wedge b}$, where a and b are constants. This is a power function.

(b) Height is the explanatory variable, and weight is the response variable. Here is a scatterplot of the data.

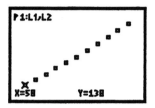

(c) Calculate the logarithms of the heights and the logarithms of the weights. Plot log(WT) vs. log(HT). The plot appears to be very linear, so least-squares regression is performed on the transformed data. The correlation is 0.99996. The regression line fits the transformed data extremely well.

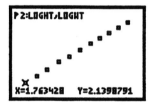 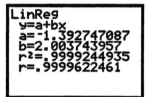 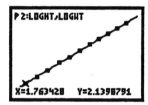

(d) Here is a residual plot for the transformed data.

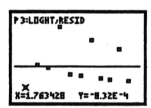

There is no discernable pattern. The line clearly fits the transformed data well.

(e) An inverse transformation yields a power equation for the original overweight data: $y = (10^{\wedge}-1.3927)(x^{\wedge}2.0037)$.

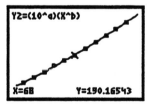

The predicted severely overweight value for a 5'10" adult (70 inches tall) would be $y = (10^{\wedge}-1.3927)(70^{\wedge}2.0037) = 201.5$ pounds. The predicted severely overweight value for a 7 foot adult (84 inches tall) would be $y = (10^{\wedge}-1.3927)(84^{\wedge}2.0037) = 290.4$ pounds.

4.5 *Solution 1.* If an exponential model is chosen and all of the data points are used, and regression is performed on the log of letter costs vs. year, the least-squares regression line is $\log \hat{y} = -54.454 + .027088x$. The correlation of the transformed points is 0.983. The inverse transformation yields $\hat{y} = (10^{-54.454})(10^{.0271x})$. When $x = 2005$, $\hat{y} = .72$. The cost will reach $.50 in the year 1999.

Solution 2. Here is another solution that offers some improvements. We begin with a scatterplot of the cost per ounce of a first class letter from 1958 to 1995. Notice that we are not using the point (1975, .10) since that date documented only an increase in postcard rates.

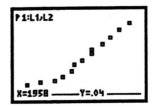

We notice that except for the first two points, the plot is fairly linear. Deleting the first two points and performing least-squares regression on the remaining points yields a correlation of 0.9955. The residual plot confirms that the LSRL is a good model.

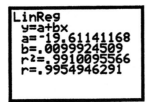 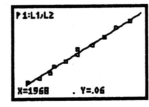 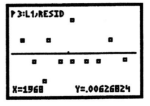

Solution 3. Using methods from this section, however, we investigate whether the growth in first class rates is exponential. Here is a plot of the log of costs (in list L_3) vs. year.

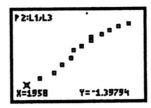

This does not show a very linear pattern, but the last 5 points, beginning with the increase in November 1981, may be linear. We will delete the first 8 points and work with the last 5 points.

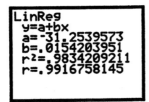 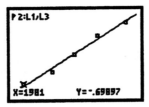 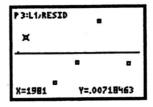

The correlation ($r = 0.99$) is high, and the residual plots shows that the line is a good model for the transformed model. Transforming back to obtain the exponential function, we obtain $\hat{y} = 10^{\wedge}(-31.2540 + .0154x)$.

This exponential model predicts a cost of \$.46 in 2005 and predicts that \$.50 will be reached in 2007. For comparison, the linear model from Solution 2 predicts a cost of \$.42 in 2005 and predicts that \$.50 will be reached in the year 2013. Which of these models you think is more accurate or reliable is a judgment call.

4.6 (a) Here is a scatterplot of the baseball average salaries from 1989 to 1997.

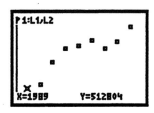

Year	Average salary	Ratio
1989	$512,804	
1990	578,930	1.129
1991	891,188	1.539
1992	1,084,408	1.217
1993	1,120,254	1.033
1994	1,188,679	1.061
1995	1,071,029	0.901
1996	1,176,967	1.099
1997	1,383,578	1.176
	Average ratio:	1.144

The 1991 salary represents a very dramatic average raise of more than 50%.

(b) The average salaries for years 1991, 1992, 1993, and 1994 seem to be out of line.

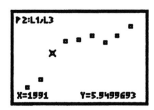

(c) After deleting the four points for 1991–1994, the plot of log SALARY vs. log YEAR appears as shown. Performing regression on the remaining 5 points gives a correlation of $r = .9995$.

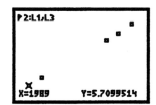 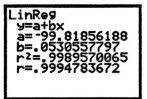 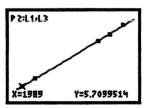

(d) Interestingly, the average salary seemed to get back "in line" after the strike, suggesting that a correction may have been needed. (e) The average salary has been higher than the median salary in recent years because a few very high salaries paid to "star" players have caused the mean to move up toward those very high salaries. The median salary, on the other hand, was resistant to the highest salaries.

4.7 (a) A scatterplot of the EFT data shows an exponential growth pattern. Calculating the ratios of current to previous transactions shows a consistent mean ratio of 1.125.

Year	Transactions	Ratio
1985	3,579	
1990	5,942	
1991	6,642	1.12
1992	7,537	1.13
1993	8,135	1.10
1994	8,958	1.10
1995	10,464	1.17
1996	11,830	1.13

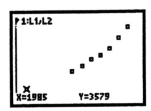

(b) A plot of log(TRANSACTIONS) vs. YEAR shows a linear pattern. Performing regression on the transformed points yields a strong correlation, $r = .998$.

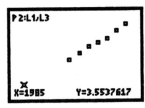 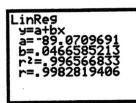 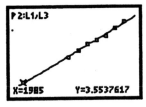 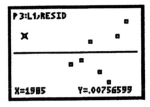

The residual plot shows no pattern, so the line is a good model for the transformed points. (c) Performing the inverse transformation produces the exponential form $y = (10^{-89.071})(10^{.0467x})$. This model predicts $y(2000) = 17{,}623$ million EFT transactions in the year 2000.

 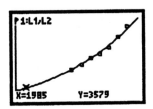

4.8 (a) Here is a scatterplot of the U.S. postage stamp production from 1848 to 1988, along with a plot of log(STAMPS) vs. YEAR.

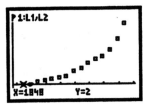 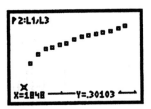

(b) Deleting the first 3 points and then regressing the remaining points gives a correlation of .996 for the transformed points.

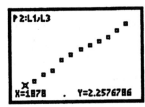 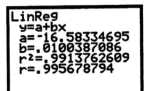 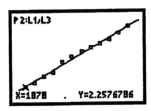

Performing the inverse transformation yields $\hat{y} = (10^{-16.5833})(10^{.01x})$. Here is the original data with the exponential function overlayed.

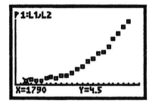

(c) This model predicts that in the year 2000, the cumulative number of U.S. stamps issued will be $\hat{y}(2,000) = 3,119$.

4.9 (a) A scatterplot of the population density (in list L_1) vs. year (in L_2) data suggests that the growth is exponential. Calculating the logs of the population (in L_3) against the year appears fairly linear, so linear regression was performed on the transformed data to obtain $\log \hat{y} = -10.8317 + .006389x$. The correlation between x and $\log y$ is .99.

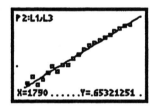 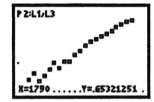 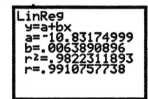

Overlaying this least-squares line on the plot of $\ln \hat{y}$ vs. x is shown. Performing the inverse transformation yields the exponential form $\hat{y} = 10^{\wedge}(-10.8317 + .006389x)$. The original scatterplot is shown with this exponential curve superimposed. The fit appears to be good.

 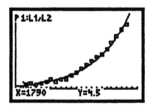

According to this model, the predicted population density in the year 2000 will be $\hat{y} = 10^{\wedge}(-10.8317 + (.00638)(2000)) = 10^{\wedge}(1.9465) = 88.4$ persons per square mile.

(b) The behavior of the population density between 1790 and 1860 is erratic, compared with the remaining years. During this period, the United States was acquiring territory, which led to an emigration from east to west and consequent periodic fluctuations in density. In particular, the Louisiana Purchase of 1803 led to the drop in population density between 1800 and 1810, due to the United States acquiring a large portion of the territory west of the Mississippi River. A similar drop can be seen between 1840 and 1850, caused by the acquisition of Mexican territory in the southwest and California as a result of the Mexican War, plus the annexation of Texas.

4.10 (a) Here is a scatterplot of expenditures per capita for health care in the United States and a plot of log(EXPENDITURES) vs. YEAR. Because the pattern appears to be linear, we regress log(EXPENDITURES) on YEAR. The correlation is .9977 for the transformed points.

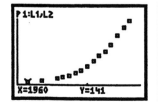 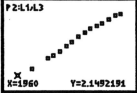 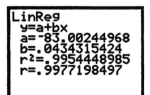 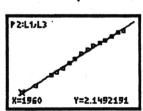

Despite the very high correlation for the transformed points, the residual plot signals some danger. It shows that the growth in health care expenditures has been slowing since 1982.

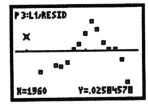 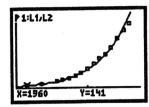

With this caveat, our exponential model takes the form $y = (10^{-83.0024})(10^{.0434x})$.

(b) Our model predicts per capita expenditures for health care in the year 2000 in the amount $7,255, more than twice the amount in 1994. The residual plot and the last plot both tell us that our prediction for 2000 is likely to be inflated.

Postscript. The residual plot tells us that something significant happened in 1982. Perhaps a new model should be fitted using only the data since 1982.

4.11 (a) A scatterplot of violent crimes vs. year shows an increasing pattern until about 1991, when the pattern starts to level out and then decline during the years 1992–1994. Also, there is a spike (greater increase than expected) in 1986.

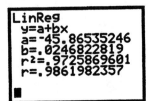

(b) Ratios:

1984 to 1985	1329/1273 = 1.04
1985 to 1986	1489/1329 = 1.12
1986 to 1987	1484/1489 = .997
1987 to 1988	1566/1484 = 1.06
1988 to 1989	1646/1566 = 1.05
1989 to 1990	1820/1646 = 1.11
1990 to 1991	1912/1820 = 1.05
1991 to 1992	1932/1912 = 1.01
1992 to 1993	1926/1932 = .997
1993 to 1994	1864/1926 = .968

Until 1992, ratios stay approximately constant, and (on average) slightly greater than 1; the average for the first 8 points is 1.05. Violent crimes are increasing exponentially, but at a very slow growth rate, between 1984 and 1991.

(c) Delete the last three points, and take logarithms of the remaining (1984–1991) violent crime numbers (y). The equation of the least-squares regression line of log y on x is log $\hat{y} = -45.865 + .02468x$. The correlation is $r = .986$. The LSRL for the transformed data is shown.

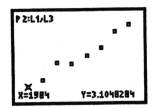 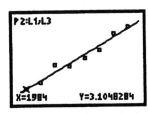

(d) Raising 10 to both sides of the equation yields the inverse transformation: $\hat{y} = 10^\wedge$ ($-45.865 + .02468x$). The exponential model fitted to the original data set is shown on page 54.

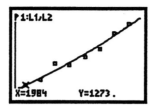

(e) The predicted number of crimes in 1986 is $\hat{y}(1986) = 10\wedge(-45.865 + (.02468)(1986)) = 10\wedge(3.152452) = 1424$. The residual for 1986 is $1484 - 1424 = 60$.

4.12 The heart weight (a 3-dimensional property) of these mammals should be proportional to the length (1-dimensional) of the cavity of the left ventricle. Here is a scatterplot of heart weight on length of left ventricle cavity.

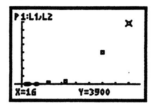

Although the scatterplot appears to be exponential, a power function model makes more sense in this setting. We therefore conjecture a model of the form WEIGHT = a $\times$ LENGTH$\wedge$b. Plotting log(WEIGHT) vs. log(LENGTH), a linear pattern of points is obtained, confirming our choice of models.

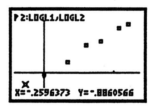

Next, linear regression is performed on the transformed points, and the LSRL is overlayed on the plot of the transformed points. The correlation is 0.997. The residual plot confirms that the power function model is appropriate.

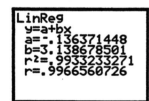 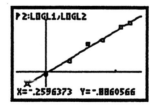 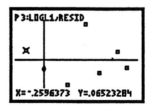

Performing the inverse transformation proceeds as follows:

$$\log \hat{y} = -.1364 + 3.1387 \log x = -.1364 + \log(x)^{3.1387}$$

$$10^{\log \hat{y}} = 10^{(-.1364 + \log(x)\,3.1387)}$$

$$\hat{y} = (10^{-.1364})(x^{3.1387})$$

The power function plotted with the original data set shows a reasonably good model for this mammal heart data.

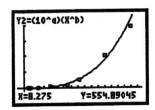

4.13 (a) Here is a scatterplot of the pizza price data (P1:L_1,L_2). If price is proportional to surface *area* of the pizza, then power regression ($y = ax^b$) should be an appropriate model, where $x =$ diameter of the pizza. On the TI-83, enter the logarithms of x in, say, list L_3, and the logs of y in list L_4. If a power function is an appropriate model, then the plot of log y on log x should be linear. Here is a plot of the transformed data (P2:L_3,L_4).

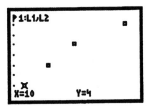
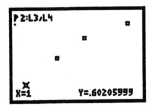

Performing least squares regression of log y vs. log x yields the following equation: log $\hat{y} = -.9172 + 1.15516$ log x. The correlation is $r = .976$. Performing the inverse transformation, we raise 10 to both sides of the equation and simplify to obtain $y = .121\ x^{1.5516}$. The last point (the 18″ giant pizza) is out of line. Perhaps this size pizza is priced lower than it should be to give greater value. If this last point is deleted, as being nonrepresentative, and least-squares regression is performed on the remaining points, the power regression model becomes $y = 10^a x^b = .0348x^{2.065}$. The power of x is very close to the 2 you would expect for an area, and the r value improves to 0.9988. This is the model we will adopt.

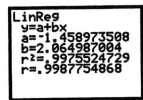
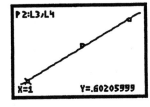

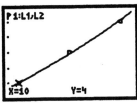

(Note that although a straight line and a logarithmic curve both fit these data better, we reject these models as inferior because of the area consideration.)

(b) Clearly, the giant pizza (18″) is underpriced. According to our model, the price of an 18″ pizza should cost $Y_2(18) = .0348(18)\text{\^{}}2.065 = 13.59$.

(c) A new 6″ pizza should cost $1.95 under the first power function model and $1.41 according to the second power model.

(d) A 24″ pizza would cost $16.76 under the first model and $24.61 under the second model.

4.14 (a) With the years (x) installed in list L_1, the times (y) in L_2, log of x in L_3, and log y in L_4, here are plots of log y on x (assuming an exponential model) as Plot1, and log y on log x (assuming a power model) as Plot2.

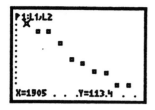 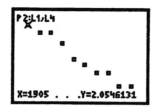 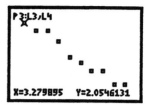

Linear regression on the transformed data for the *exponential* model (log y on x) produces the equation $\log \hat{y} = 3.141 - .00057x$. The correlation is $r = .9839$.

 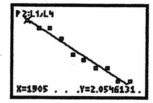 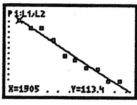

Linear regression on the transformed data for the *power* model (log y on x) produces the equation $\log \hat{y} = 10.4514 - 2.5598 \log x$. The correlation is $r = .9843$.

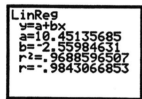 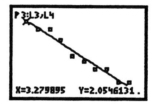 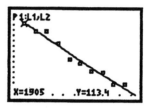

Based on the correlation value, the power model would yield a better fit. The power model would take the form $\hat{y} = (10^{\wedge}10.4514)(x^{\wedge}-2.5598)$.

(b) The scatterplot for the women's times is shown. For the exponential model: regression for log y on x yields $\log \hat{y} = 5.1203 - .001544x$ and correlation $-.9737$. For the power model: regression for log y on log x yields $\log \hat{y} = 25.0506 - 6.9727 \log x$ and correlation $-.9747$. Again, a power model for the women's times appears slightly better, by virtue of a slightly higher correlation. It would take the form $\hat{y} = (10^{\wedge}25.050)(x^{\wedge}-6.9727)$.

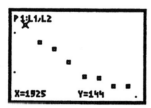 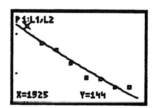

(c) Neither curve will eventually reach 0, at least not in the next 1 million years. It is true that the women's times are decreasing faster than the men's in the years 1925 to 1995, suggesting that the curves will intersect in the future. The power curves from our models do intersect in year 2033; the common record would then be 96.13 seconds. Extrapolation is dangerous, of course, and whether the women will overtake the men is open to speculation.

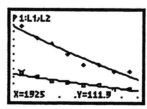 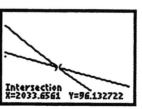

(d) Both power models appear to be reasonably good models.

4.15 *Notes:* (1) Students should observe that winning in this game is a function of (depends on) the area of the disk used, and that the area of the disk is a function of the square of the diameter. Thus one would expect a power function model, with the leading exponent a number near 2. We will force a quadratic curve fit. (2) Although the activity is presented in terms of 9 or 12 inch tile squares, it is recommended that diameters of disks be recorded in millimeters, because the analysis will be easier. (3) Your results should be *similar* to the results below.

(a) Here are some *representative* results:

Type of Disk	Diameter (mm)	No. of winners/ no. of tosses	Winning relative frequency
Dime	18	80/100	.80
Quarter	24	76/100	.76
Baking powder lid	66	47/100	.47
Hershey's syrup lid	78	46/100	.46
Regular (13 oz) coffee	104	33/100	.33
Lipton iced tea mix lid	132	20/100	.20
Large (39 oz) coffee lid	158	9/100	.09

(b) A scatterplot of winning percent on disk diameter should look something like this:

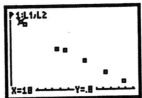

As disk diameter increases, the relative frequency of winning decreases. (The larger the disk, the harder it is to have it land completely within a square tile.)

(c) Entering the disk diameters in list L_1 and the winning percents in list L_2, and using the TI-83's quadratic regression on these data (STAT / CALC / 5:QuadReg) produces the following:

Here is the scatterplot with the quadratic function model.

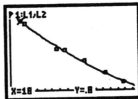

The model appears to fit the data very well.

(d) $y(0)$ should equal 1. As the diameter of the disk gets smaller and smaller, the winning relative frequency gets larger and larger, and in the extreme case of zero diameter, the relative frequency should be 1. If a disk has diameter equal to or greater than the dimension of the tile square, the relative frequency of wins should be 0.

4.16 (a) If the center of the disk is in the unshaded area, the disk will cross an edge.

$$y = \text{winning percentage} = \frac{\text{area of shaded square}}{\text{area of tile}}$$

$$y = \frac{(229 - d)^2}{229^2} = \frac{229^2 - 458 + d^2}{229^2}$$

$$y = .000019\, d^2 - .0087\, d + 1$$

This is the analytical (theoretical) model for this game of chance. From this equation, $y(0) = 1$. According to this model, when the winning relative frequency $y = .40$, the diameter $x = 84.6$, using the TI-83's CALC function.

(c) When $y = .35$, $x = 94.0$.

4.17 (a)

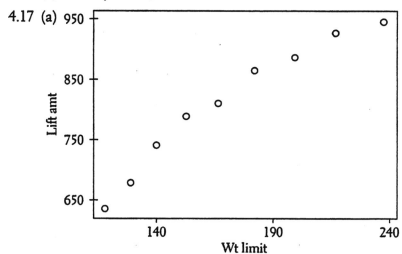

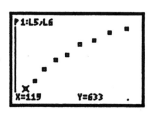

There is a clear positive association between weight limit and lift amount. As weight limit increases, the rate of increase of weight limit appears to "flatten out."

(b) The quadratic regression option yields the model

$$y = -.0163x^2 + 8.41x - 132.984$$

where $x =$ weight limit and $y =$ lift amount. The predicted values of y at the values of x listed in the table are: 636.9817, 684.846, 728.7657, 775.5852, 818.374, 860.1753, 897.1957, 925.7548, 945.2988. The data fit the model reasonably well.

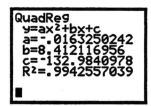
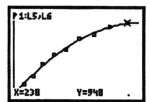
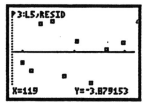

(c) At $x = 0$, the model yields $y = -132.984$, a negative number. At $x = 300$, the model yields $y = 923.016$. A weight that is *less* than the corresponding lift amounts predicted for weight limits of 218 and 238 pounds. These results suggest that the model is appropriate only within the prescribed weight limits of 119–238 pounds. The model reaches its maximum value of y at an x between 238 and 300, and to use the model for x larger than this number would be inappropriate, obviously. The model is also inappropriate for very small weight limits, since one must be a certain weight in order to be a weight lifter in the first place!

(d) If x and y are measured in kilograms instead of pounds, the coefficient of x^2 and the constant term in the model would change, but the coefficient of the linear (x) term would not.

4.18 (a) Plot1 shows electrical usage vs. house size. Plot2 shows log (electrical usage) on log (house size). The scatterplot suggests a power (quadratic?) model, but the plot of log y on log x does not show a linear trend.

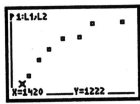 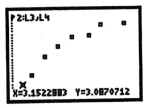

This tells us that $y = ax^b$ is not a suitable model. But perhaps a general quadratic function of the form $y = ax^2 + bx + c$ would be useful. Specifying quadratic regression (STAT / CALC / 5:QuadReg) produces the following generalized model, and overlaying the parabola on the scatterplot shows a reasonably good fit, with the exception of one low point.

 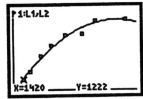

Extrapolation to smaller homes might be acceptable because the curve is fairly straight for the first 4 or 5 points, but extrapolating to larger house sizes would not make sense. Because the curve has clearly peaked at about 2700 square-feet, that would suggest, for example, that a 3300 square-foot house would use about the same amount of electricity as a 1980 square-foot house, and that defies common sense.

SECTION 4.2

4.19 (a) Regression line: $\hat{y} = 1166.93 - 0.58679x$. (b) Based on the slope, the farm population decreased about 590 thousand (0.59 million) people per year. The regression line explains 97.7% of the variation. (c) $-782{,}100$ — clearly a ridiculous answer, since a population must be greater than or equal to 0.

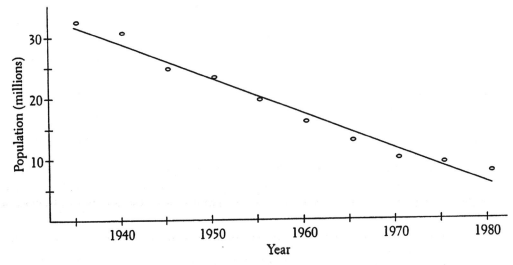

4.20 The explanatory and response variables were "consumption of herbal tea" and "cheerfulness." The most important lurking variable is social interaction — many of the nursing home residents may have been lonely before the students started visiting.

4.21 The correlation would be smaller because there is much more variation among the individual data points. This variation could not be as fully explained by the linear relationship between speed and step rate.

4.22 Seriousness of the fire is a lurking variable: more serious fires require more attention. It would be more accurate to say that a large fire "causes" more firefighters to be sent, rather than vice versa.

4.23 Age is the lurking variable here: we would expect both quantities — shoe size and reading level — to increase as a child ages.

4.24 No; more likely it means that patients with more serious conditions (which require longer stays) tend to go to larger hospitals, which are more likely to have the facilities to treat those problems.

4.25 (a) $r^2 = 0.925$ — more than 90% of the variation in one SAT score can be explained through a linear relationship with the other score. (b) The correlation would be much smaller, since individual students have much more variation between their scores. Some may have greater verbal skills and low scores in math (or vice versa); some will be strong in both areas, and some will be weak in both areas. By averaging — or, as in this case, taking the median of — the scores of large groups of students, we muffle the effects of these individual variations.

4.26 The plot below is a very simplified (and not very realistic) example — open circles are economists in business; filled circles are teaching economists. The plot should show positive association when either set of circles is viewed separately, and should show a large number of bachelor's degree economists in business, and graduate degree economists in academia.

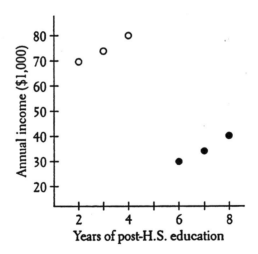

4.27 The explanatory variable is whether or not a student has taken at least two years of foreign language, and the score on the test is the response. The lurking variable is the students' English skills *before* taking (or not taking) the foreign language: students who have a good command of English early in their high school career are more likely to choose (or be advised to choose) to take a foreign language.

4.28 Social status is a possible lurking variable: children from upper-class families can more easily afford higher education, and they would typically have had better preparation for college as well. They may also have some advantages when seeking employment, and have more initial money should they want to start their own business.

This could be compounded by racial distinctions: prejudicial hiring practices may keep minorities out of higher-paying positions.

It also could be that some causation goes the other way: a man who is doing well in his job might be encouraged to pursue further education.

4.29 Apparently drivers are typically larger and heavier men than conductors — and are therefore more predisposed to health problems such as heart disease.

SECTION 4.3

4.30 Column sums to 73,026, which differs by 2 (thousand) from the total given. Roundoff error accounts for the difference.

4.31 24.9%, 43.9%, and 31.3% (total is 100.1% due to rounding).

4.32 (a) 5375. (b) 1004/5375 = 18.7%. (c) Both parents smoke: 1780 (33.1%); one parent smokes: 2239 (41.7%); neither parent smokes: 1356 (25.2%).

4.33 12.9%, 12.5%, and 30.8%. The percentage of people who did not finish high school is about the same for the 25–34 and 35–54 age groups, but more than doubles for the 55 and over age group.

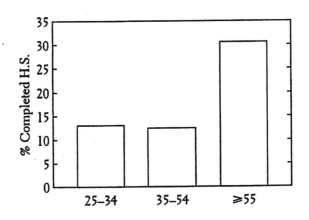

4.34 Compute 16,035/52,022 = 30.8%, 18,320/52,022 = 35.2%, etc.

4.35 Among 35 to 54 year-olds: 12.5% never finished high school, 33.0% finished high school, 27.3% had some college, and 27.2% completed college. This is more like the 25–34 age group than the 55 and over group.

4.36 Among those with 4 or more years of college: 27.1% are 25–34, 52.0% are 35–54, and 20.9% are 55 or older.

4.37 Two possible answers: Row 1–30, 20; Row 2–30, 20; and Row 1–10, 40; Row 2–50, 0.

4.38 (a) 6014; 1.26%. (b) Blood pressure is explanatory. (c) Yes: among those with low blood pressure, 0.785% died; the death rate in the high blood pressure group was 1.65% — about twice as high as the other group.

4.39 (a) Of students with two smoking parents, 22.5% smoke; with one smoking parent, the percentage drops to 18.6%; with no smoking parents, only 13.9% of the students smoke. (b) On page 61. (c) It appears that children of smokers are more likely to smoke — even more so when both parents are smokers.

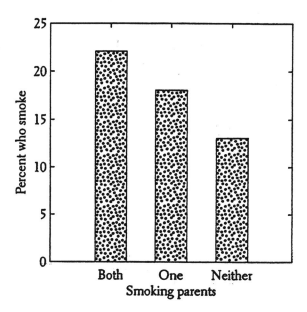

4.40 (a) Below. (b) 70% of male applicants are admitted, while only 56% of females are admitted. (c) 80% of male business school applicants are admitted, compared with 90% of females; in the law school, 10% of males are admitted, compared with 33.3% of females. (d) Six out of 7 men apply to the business school, which admits 83% of all applicants, while 3 of 5 women apply to the law school, which only admits 27.5% of its applicants.

	Admit	Deny
Male	490	210
Female	280	220

4.41 (a) Below. (b) Overall, 11.9% of white defendants and 10.2% of black defendants get the death penalty. However, for white victims, the percentages are 12.6% and 17.5% (respectively); when the victim is black, they are 0% and 5.8%. (c) In cases involving white victims, 14% of defendants got the death penalty; when the victim was black, only 5.4% of defendants were sentenced to death. White defendants killed whites 94.3% of the time — but are less likely to get the death penalty than blacks who killed whites.

	Yes	No
White Defendant	19	141
Black Defendant	17	149

4.42 (a) 704,000. (b) 2,065,000. (c) Roundoff error.

4.43 (a) 11,374,000. (b) 51.2%. (c) 60.8%, 22.1%, 68.4%, and 11.0%. Bar chart on page 62. (d) The 18–21 age group makes up more than 60% of full-time students, but comprises less than 20% of part-time students.

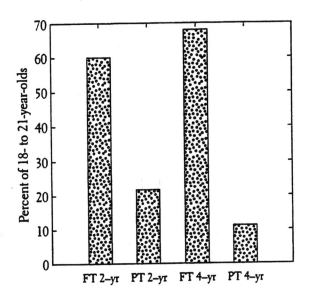

4.44 (a) 34.1%. (b) 36.9%.

4.45 (a) Counts: 127, 5829, 3031, 1907, 480. Percents: 1.1%, 51.2%, 26.6%, 16.8%, 4.2%. (b) 0.2%, 22.1%, 33.4%, 34.1%, and 10.1%. (c) The biggest difference between the distributions in (a) and (b) is that among part-time students at 2-year colleges, there is a markedly lower percentage of 18- to 21-year-olds, and considerable increases in the higher age brackets — the last two age categories are more than twice as large in (b) as they were in (a).

4.46 (a) 7.2%. (b) 10.1% of the restrained children were injured, compared to 15.4% of unrestrained children.

4.47

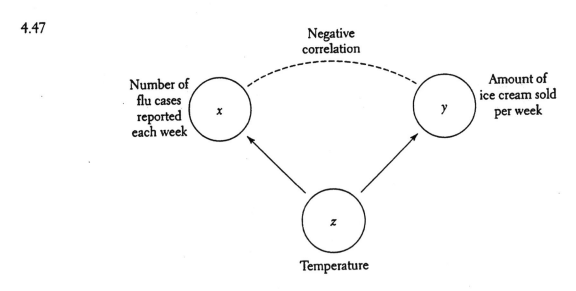

Both x and y are responding to the variable $z = temperature$. In the winter, when temperatures are low, there are many flu cases (x) but relatively little ice cream sold (y). In the summer, when temperatures are high, there are few cases of flu, but a large amount of ice cream is sold. This is an example of *common response*.

4.48

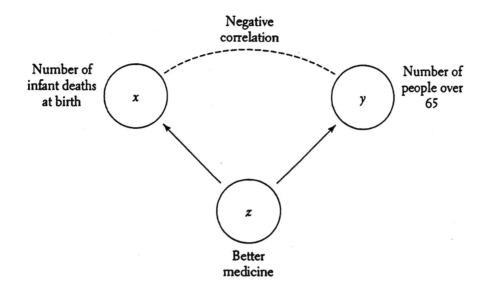

In the past 30 years, improving medical knowledge, technology, and level of care have resulted in fewer infant deaths at birth (x). Better medicine (and healthier lifestyles) have enabled people to live longer, so the number of people over 65 (y) has increased. Both variables, x and y, are responding to a third variable, z = better medicine. This is an example of common response.

4.49 (a) 59.0%. (b) Larger businesses were less likely to respond: only 37.5% of the small businesses did not respond, compared to 59.5% of medium-sized businesses and 80% of large businesses. (c) Bar chart below.

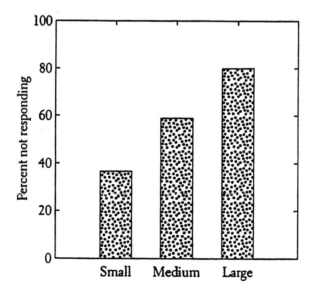

4.50 (a) On page 64. (b) Joe: .240, Moe: .260. Moe has the best overall batting average. (c) Against right-handed pitchers: Joe: .400, Moe: .300. Against left-handed pitchers: Joe: .200, Moe: .100. Joe is better against both kinds of pitchers. (d) Both players do better against right-handed pitchers than against left-handed pitchers. Joe spent 80% of his at-bats facing left-handers, while Moe only faced left-handers 20% of the time.

	Hit	No hit
All pitchers		
Joe	120	380
Moe	130	370
Right-handed		
Joe	40	60
Moe	120	280
Left-handed		
Joe	80	320
Moe	10	90

CHAPTER REVIEW

4.51 $2^{1\times4} = 16$, $2^{5\times4} = 1,048,576$.

4.52 (a) 1, 2, 4, 8, 16, 32, 64, 128, 256, 512.

(b)

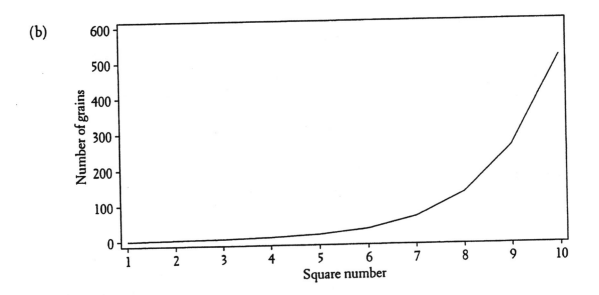

(c) Approximately 9,000,000,000,000,000,000.

(d) 0.00, 0.30, 0.60, 0.90, 1.20, 1.51, 1.81, 2.11, 2.41, 2.71.

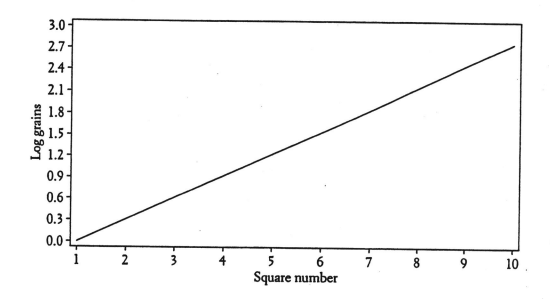

(e) $b = .3$, $a = -.3$, $-.3 + .3(64) = 18.9$. The log of the answer in part (c) is 18.95.

4.53 (a) $y = 500(1.075)^{year}$. 537.50, 577,81, 621.15, 667.73, 717.81, 771.65, 829.52, 891.74, 958.62, 1030.52.

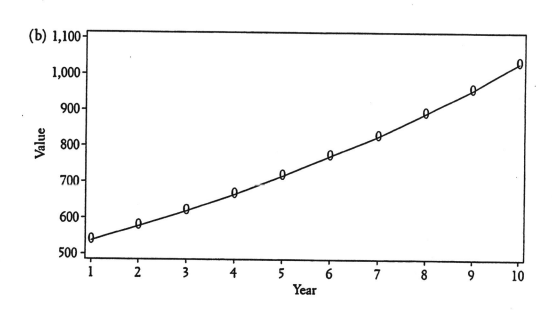

(c) The logs are 2.73, 2.76, 2.79, 2.82, 2.86, 2.89, 2.92, 2.95, 2.98, 3.01.

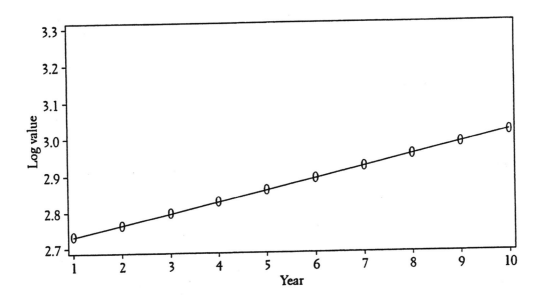

4.54 Alice has $500(1.075)^{25} = 3049.17$, Fred has $500 + 100(25) = 3000.00$.

4.55 (a) The pattern appears to be exponential.

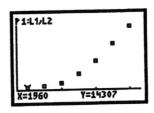

(b) The plot of log SPENDING vs. YEAR appears linear, so the exponential growth model fits well.

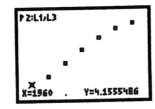 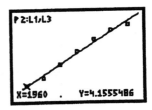

(d) Predicted log for 1988 is 5.617046, predicted amount spent in 1988 is $414,043.74.

(e) Log is 5.55. The point is somewhat below the line. The rate of growth appears to be slower.

4.56 (a)

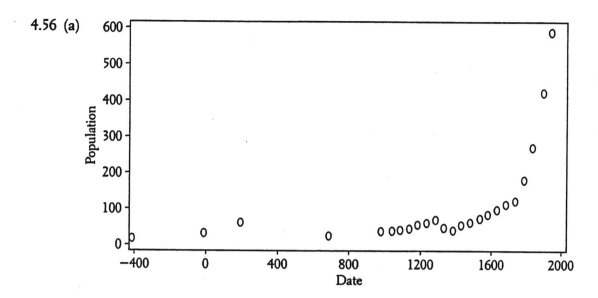

(b)

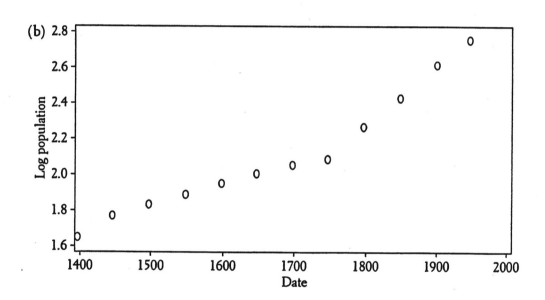

The ratios of consecutive terms between 1400 and 1950 are:

Years	Ratio	Years	Ratio
1400 to 1450	1.33	1700 to 1750	1.09
1450 to 1500	1.15	1750 to 1800	1.50
1500 to 1550	1.13	1800 to 1850	1.47
1550 to 1600	1.15	1850 to 1900	1.54
1600 to 1650	1.14	1900 to 1950	1.40
1650 to 1700	1.12		

(c) The plot of log (population) vs. date suggests that the growth between 1400 and 1950 cannot be described by one exponential function. The growth from 1400 to 1750 was exponential with one rate, and the growth from 1750 to 1950 was exponential with another rate. We will use only the data from 1750 to 1950. Plot1 shows the original data from those years, and Plot2 shows the transformed data.

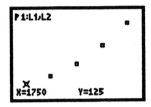 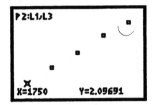

Least-squares regression is performed on the transformed data, with a correlation of .999.

(d) The equation of the line is $\log \hat{y} = -3.8792 + .0034x$. The inverse transformation is then $10^{\wedge}(\log \hat{y}) = 10^{\wedge}(-3.8792 + .0034x)$ or $\hat{y} = (10^{-3.8792})\, 10^{.0034x}$. Here is the exponential model with the 1750 to 1950 data:

 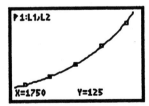

The growth of population during this period is almost perfectly exponential.

(e) The test for exponential growth was restricted to the period from 1400 to 1950 because prior to 1400 there were several major events that interrupted population growth. In fact, because there were clearly two distinct exponential patterns between 1400 and 1950, the decision was made to restrict attention further to the period 1750 to 1950.

4.57 (a) The plot of population vs. year suggests exponential growth.

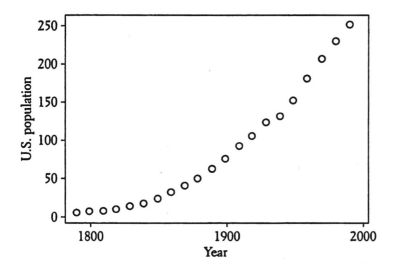

(b) Here is a plot of log (population) vs. year.

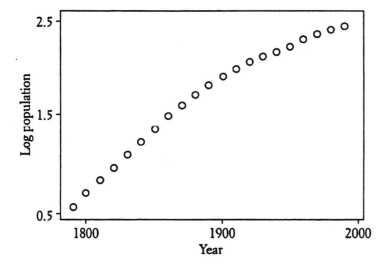

The expert's opinion is borne out by the fact that the slope of the linear relationship between log (population) and year appears to decrease slightly beginning at around $x = 1880$. This reflects a lower exponential growth rate.

(c) Here is a plot of log (population) vs. year for 1900 to 1990.

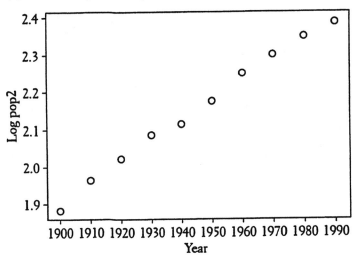

Least-squares regression of log (population) vs. year is requested from Minitab. Here are the results:

```
The regression equation is
LOG POP2 = − 8.86 + 0.00566 YEAR6

Predictor        Coef        Stdev    t-ratio       p
Constant      -8.8605       0.2883     -30.73   0.000
YEAR  6     0.0056645    0.0001482      38.21   0.000

s  =  0.01346     R-sq = 99.5%     R-sq(adj) = 99.4%
```

Using only this data, we obtain the following least-squares model from Minitab:

$$\log \hat{y} = -8.8605 + .0055665x$$

The inverse transformation yields the result:

$$\hat{y} = (10^{-8.8605})(10^{.0055665x})$$

(d) When $x = 2000$, $y = 10^{2.4685} = 294.1$ million.

4.58 A plot of the data (P1) reveals what appears to be exponential growth. Plotting log (productivity) against year (P2) shows a linear pattern.

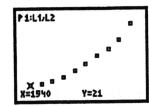   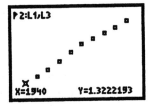

Performing least-squares regression on the transformed points yields the equation $\hat{y} = -43.0817 + .0229x$.

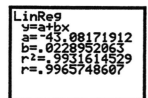

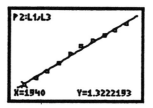

While the residual plot (P3) clearly shows periodic oscillations, that phenomenon is frequently observed when studying effects of nature, especially in agriculture. We note this weakness in the model and continue.

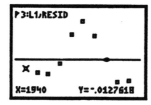

The inverse transformation gives the exponential model:

$$10^{\wedge}\log \hat{y} = 10^{\wedge}(-43.0817 + .0229x)$$

or

$$\hat{y} = (10^{-43.0817})(10^{.0229x})$$

The exponential model adequately captures the trend of the data.

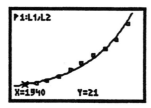

4.59 (a) The scatterplot appears somewhat linear. Least-squares regression on the data produces a LSRL with correlation .988. There is a negative association. As year increases, infant mortality decreases.

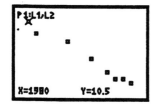
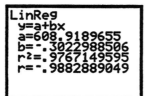
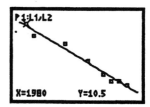

(b) Contemplating an exponential fit, common ratios were calculated. The ratio for 1980 to 1981 is .924; the ratio for 1990 to 1991 is .944; the ratio for 1991 to 1992 is 1; the ratio for 1992 to 1993 is .956. Although these ratios seem to be growing, they are not sequential because mortality data is missing for certain years. We plot log (mortality) vs. year and perform least-squares regression. The results are as shown along with a plot of the transformed data and the LSRL on page 72.

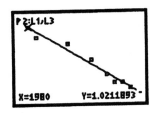 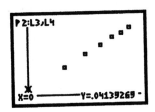

The exponential model has equation $\hat{y} = 10\wedge(32.3563 - .0158x)$.

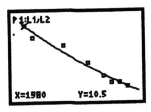

(c) Using the exponential model, $\hat{y} = (10^{32.3563})(10^{-.0158x})$, the following infant mortality rates are predicted for the years 1994 to 99: 6.30, 6.07, 5.85, 5.64, 5.44, and 5.25. This (exponential decay) model should not be used to predict infant mortality out to the year 2005.

4.60 (a) The scatterplot (P1) of period vs. length of pendulum suggests a power function model. The plot (P2) of log (period) vs. log (length) appears linear. There is a positive association; as length increases, the period increases.

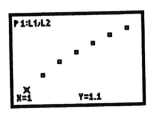 

(b) Least-squares regression is performed on the transformed data. The correlation between the transformed variables is extremely strong. The LSRL fits the transformed data like a glove.

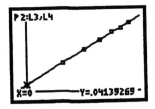 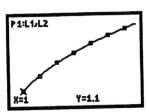

The power function model takes the form $\hat{y} = (10^{.0415})(x^{.5043})$.

(c) The equation for the model says that the period of a pendulum is proportional to the square root of its length.

4.61 (a)

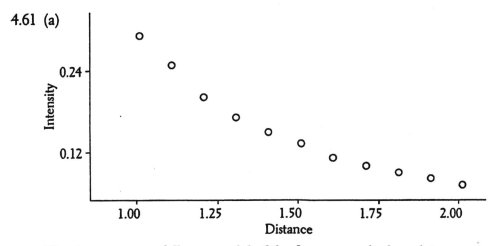

The data appear to follow a model of the form $y = ax^b$ where b is some negative number. Taking logs of both sides of this model equation, we have

$$\log y = \log a + \log x^b$$
$$= \log a + b (\log x)$$

We perform linear regression on the $\log x$ and $\log y$ data and obtain the following least-squares regression model:

$$\log y = -.5235 - 2.013 \log x$$

The inverse transformation yields

$$y = (10^{-.5235}) (x^{-2.013})$$
$$= -3 \, x^{-2.013}$$

(b) $y = 0.3 \, x^{-2.013}$ (c) The intensity of the light bulb appears to vary inversely with (approximately) the square of the distance from the bulb. (d) The formula for intensity as a function of distance is given by $y = 900/x^2$ where y is measured in *candlepower*, x in meters. With an appropriate units change to candelas, this formula appears to fit the experimental data.

4.62 In the aspirin group, 1.26% had heart attacks (0.09% were fatal, 1.17% were not), and 1.08% had strokes. Among those who took placebos, 2.17% had heart attacks (0.24% fatal, 1.93% non-fatal), and 0.89% suffered from strokes. Based on these numbers, it appears that the aspirin group had a slight advantage in heart attacks, but was possibly worse in incidence of stroke. In spite of the word "study" in the name, this was an experiment, where the doctors could not choose for themselves which pill they took. Thus, a cause-and-effect relationship seems to be indicated — but we must be careful not to apply the results too broadly. The study involved *healthy, male doctors over 40*; the same outcomes might not be observed for (e.g.) a person who already has heart problems, or a woman, or a patient under age 40.

4.63 80% of all suicide victims were men — that in itself is a major difference. Firearms were the most common method for both sexes: 65.9% of male suicides used firearms, as did 42.1% of females. Poison was a close second for women at 35.6%, compared with only 13.0% for men. In the last two categories, the percentages were pretty close: Men chose hanging 14.9% of the time, and women chose it 12.2% of the time; 6.2% of men and 10.1% of women fell into the "other" group.

4.64 (a) 58.3% of desipramine users did not have a relapse, while 25.0% of lithium users and 16.7% of those who received placebos succeeded in breaking their addictions. (b) Because the addicts were assigned randomly to their treatments, we can *tentatively* assume causation (though there are other questions we need to consider before we can reach that conclusion).

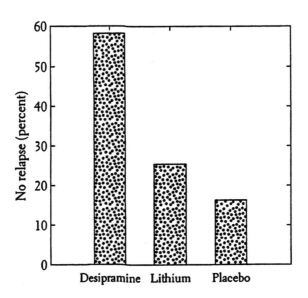

4.65 (a) 12,625; roundoff error. (b) 19.3%, 59.3%, 11.8%, and 9.6%. (c) 18–24: 71.3%, 26.5%, 0.06%, 2.0%. 40–64: 5.8%, 72.5%, 7.6%, 14.1%. Among the younger women, almost three-fourths have not yet married, and those that are married have had little time to become widowed or divorced. Most of the older group is or has been married — only about 6% are still single. (d) 48.6% of single women are 18–24, 35.9% are 25–39, 10.7% are 40–64, and 4.9% are 65 or older.

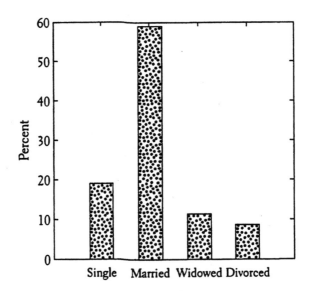

4.66 Apparently women are more likely to be in fields which pay less overall (to both men and women). For example, if many women, and few men, have Job A, where they earn $40,000 per year, and meanwhile few women and many men have Job B earning $50,000 per year, then lumping all women and men together leads to an incorrect perception of unfairness.

4.67 One simple possibility is shown below, using 7 smokers and 13 nonsmokers. Lumped together, we find that 4 of 10 overweight people die early, while 5 of 10 from the non-overweight group die early.

Early death?	Smoker		Non-smoker	
	Overweight?		Overweight?	
	Yes	No	Yes	No
Yes	1	4	3	1
No	0	2	6	3

5

Producing Data

SECTION 5.1

5.1 The population is employed adult women, the sample is the 48 club members who returned the survey.

5.2 (a) An individual is a person; the population is all adult U.S. residents. (b) An individual is a household; the population is all U.S. households. (c) An individual is a voltage regulator; the population is all the regulators in the last shipment.

5.3 Only persons with a strong opinion on the subject — strong enough that they are willing to spend the time, and 50 cents — will respond to this advertisement.

5.4 Letters to legislators are an example of a voluntary response sample — the proportion of letters opposed to the insurance should not be assumed to be a fair representation of the attitudes of the congresswoman's constituents.

5.5 Starting with 01 and numbering down the columns, one chooses 04-Bonds, 10-Fleming, 17-Liao, 19-Naber, 12-Goel, and 13-Gomez.

5.6 Starting with 01 and numbering down the columns, one chooses 19-Liang, 26-Rodriguez, 06-Castillo, and 09-Gonzalez.

5.7 Labeling from 001 to 440, we select 400, 077, 172, 417, 350, 131, 211, 273, 208, and 074.

5.8 Assign 01 to 30 to the students (in alphabetical order). The exact selection will depend on the starting line chosen in Table B; starting on line 123 gives 08-Ghosh, 15-Jones, 07-Fisher, and 27-Shaw. Assigning 0–9 to the faculty members gives (from line 109) 3-Gupta and 6-Moore. (We could also number faculty from 01 to 10, but this requires looking up 2-digit numbers.)

5.9 Label the 500 midsize accounts from 001 to 500, and the 4400 small accounts from 0001 to 4400. We first encounter numbers 417, 494, 322, 247, and 097 for the midsize group, then 3698, 1452, 2605, 2480, and 3716 for the small group.

5.10 (a) Households without telephones, or with unlisted numbers. Such households would likely be made up of poor individuals (who cannot afford a phone), those who choose not to have phones, and those who do not wish to have their phone number published. (b) Those with unlisted numbers would be included in the sampling frame when a random-digit dialer is used.

5.11 The higher no-answer was probably the second period — more families are likely to be gone for vacations, etc. Nonresponse of this type might underrepresent those who are more affluent (and are able to travel).

5.12 Form A would draw the higher negative response. It is phrased to produce a negative reaction: "giving huge sums of money" versus "contributing," and giving "to candidates" rather than "to campaigns." Also, form B presents both sides of the issue, allowing for special interest groups to have "a right to contribute."

5.13 The increased sample size gives more accurate information about the population (for example, a more accurate estimate of how many voters favor Candidate A over Candidate B).

5.14 The population is words in novels by Tom Wolfe; the sample is the first 250 words on the randomly selected page in the randomly selected novel. The variable is the length of a word.

5.15 (a) An individual is a small business; the specific population is "eating and drinking establishments" in the large city. (b) An individual is an adult; the Congressman's constituents are the *desired* population; the letter-writers are a voluntary sample and do not represent that population well. (c) Individual: auto insurance claim; the population is all the auto insurance claims filed in a given month.

5.16 Hite's questionnaires were distributed through women's groups, and thus could not include women who don't belong to such groups. Furthermore, since response was voluntary, the sample is probably biased toward those with strong feelings on the subjects. Thus, Hite's reported percentages are likely to be higher than the true percentages for the whole population of adult American women.

5.17 The call-in poll is faulty in part because it is a voluntary sample. Furthermore, even a small charge like 50 cents can discourage some people from calling in — especially poor people. Reagan's Republican policies appealed to upper-class voters, who would be less concerned about a 50 cent charge than lower-class voters who might favor Carter.

5.18 The interviewers would only get responses at households where someone was home during normal working hours. People in such households are more likely to have time to bake bread.

5.19 Number the bottles across the rows from 01 to 25, then select 12-B0986, 04-A1101, and 11-A2220. (*Note:* If numbering is done down columns instead, the sample will be A1117, B1102, and A1098.)

5.20 The blocks are already marked; select three-digit numbers and ignore those that do not appear on the map. This gives 214, 313, 409, 306, and 511.

5.21 (a) False — if it were true, then after looking at 39 digits, we would know whether or not the 40th digit was a 0, contrary to property 2. (b) True — there are 100 pairs of digits 00 through 99, and all are equally likely. (c) False — 0000 is just as likely as any other string of four digits.

5.22 (a) Split the 200 addresses into 5 groups of 40 each. Looking for 2-digit numbers from 01 to 40, we find 35, and so take 35, 75, 115, 155, and 195. (b) Every address has a 1-in-40 chance of being selected, *but* not every subset has an equal chance of being picked — for example, 01, 02, 03, 04, and 05 cannot be selected by this method.

5.23 It is *not* an SRS. In order to be an SRS, every possible sample of 250 must have an equal chance of being chosen, and this is not the case — a group consisting of 250 female engineers will not be picked, for example.

5.24 (a) This question will likely elicit more responses against gun control (that is, more people will choose 2). The two options presented are too extreme; no middle position on gun control is allowed. (b) The phrasing of this question will tend to make people respond in favor of a nuclear freeze. Only one side of the issue is presented. (c) The wording is too technical for many people to understand — and for those that *do* understand it, it is slanted because it suggests reasons why one should support recycling. It could be rewritten to something like: "Do you support economic incentives to promote recycling?"

5.25 A smaller sample gives less information about the population. "Men" constituted only about one-third of our sample, so we know less about that group than we know about all adults.

SECTION 5.2

5.26 It is not an experiment: the political scientist is merely observing a characteristic (party preference) of a group of subjects. Sex is explanatory, and the party voted for in the last election is the response variable.

5.27 (a) The liners are the experimental units. (b) The heat applied to the liners is the factor; the levels are 250°F, 275°F, 300°F, and 325°F. (c) The force required to open the package is the response variable.

5.28 (a) This is an experiment, since the teacher imposes treatments (instruction method). (b) The explanatory variable is the method used (computer software or standard curriculum), and the response is the change in reading ability.

5.29 (a) The experimental units are the batches of the product; the yield of each batch is the response variable. (b) There are two factors: temperature (with 2 levels) and stirring rates (with 3 levels), for a total of 6 treatments. (c) Since two experimental units will be used for each treatment, we need 12.

		Factor B: Stirring rates		
		60 rpm	90 rpm	120 rpm
Factor A:	50°C	1	2	3
Temperature	60°C	4	5	6

5.30 (a) In a serious case, when the patient has little chance of surviving, a doctor might choose not to recommend surgery; it might be seen as an unnecessary measure, bringing expense and a hospital stay with little benefit to the patient.

(b)

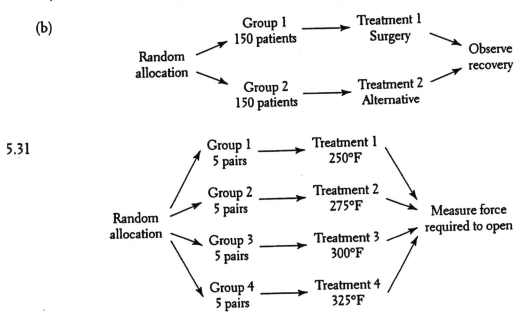

5.31

5.32 (a) Randomly select 20 women for Group 1, which will see the "childcare" version of Company B's brochure, and assign the other 20 women to Group 2 (the "no childcare" group). Allow all women to examine the appropriate brochures, and observe which company they choose. Compare the number from Group 1 who choose Company B with the corresponding number from Group 2. (b) Numbering from 01 to 40, Group 1 is 05-Cansico, 32-Roberts, 19-Hwang, 04-Brown, 25-Lippman, 29-Ng, 20-Iselin,

16-Gupta, 37-Turing, 39-Williams, 31-Rivera, 18-Howard, 07-Cortez, 13-Garcia, 33-Rosen, 02-Adamson, 36-Travers, 23-Kim, 27-McNeill, and 35-Thompson.

5.33 Number the liners from 01 to 20, then take Group 1 to be 16, 04, 19, 07, and 10; Group 2 is 13, 15, 05, 09, and 08; Group 3 is 18, 03, 01, 06, and 11. The others are in Group 4.

5.34 Randomly assign 6 students to each of Groups 1, 2, 3, 4, 5, and 6 (place the first 6 selected students in Group 1, the next 6 in Group 2, and so on). Each group will watch the version of the television show with the corresponding treatment (as numbered in Figure 5.2). Then observe their responses to the questions about their attitude toward the product, etc.

Group 1 is students 05, 16, 17, 20, 16, and 32; Group 2 is 04, 25, 29, 31, 18, and 07; Group 3 is 13, 33, 02, 36, 23, and 27; Group 4 is 35, 21, 26, 08, 10, and 11; Group 5 is 15, 12, 14, 09, 24, and 22; the rest are in Group 6.

5.35 If this year is considerably different in some way from last year, we cannot compare electricity consumption over the two years. For example, if this summer is warmer, the customers may run their air conditioners more often. The possible differences between the two years would confound the effects of the treatments.

5.36 The second design is an experiment—a treatment is imposed on the subjects. The first is a study; it may be confounded by the types of men in each group. In spite of the researcher's attempt to match "similar" men from each group, those in the first group (who exercise) could be somehow different from men in the non-exercising group.

5.37 There almost certainly was *some* difference between the sexes and between blacks and whites; the difference between men and women was so large that it is unlikely to be due to chance. For black and white students, however, the difference was small enough that it could be attributed to random variation.

5.38 Because the experimenter knew which subjects had learned the meditation techniques, he (or she) may have had some expectations about the outcome of the experiment: if the experimenter believed that meditation was beneficial, he may subconsciously rate that group as being less anxious.

5.39 (a) If only the new drug is administered, and the subjects are then interviewed, their responses will not be useful, because there will be nothing to compare them to: How much "pain relief" does one expect to experience? (b) Randomly assign 20 patients to each of three groups: Group 1, the placebo group; Group 2, the aspirin group; and Group 3, which will receive the new medication. After treating the patients, ask them how much pain relief they feel, and then compare the average pain relief experienced by each group. (c) The subjects should certainly not know what drug they are getting—a patient told that she is receiving a placebo, for example, will probably not expect any pain relief. (d) Yes— presumably, the researchers would like to conclude that the new medication is better than aspirin. If it is not double-blind, the interviewers may subtly influence the subjects into giving responses that support that conclusion.

5.40 (a) Ordered by increasing weight, the five blocks are (1) Williams-22, Deng-24, Hernandez-25, and Moses-25; (2) Santiago-27, Kendall-28, Mann-28, and Smith-29; (3) Brunk-30, Obrach-30, Rodriguez-30, and Loren-32; (4) Jackson-33, Stall-33, Brown-34, and Cruz-34; (5) Birnbaum-35, Tran-35, Nevesky-39, and Wilansky-42. (b) The exact randomization will vary with the starting line in Table B. Different methods are possible; perhaps the simplest is to number from 1 to 4 within each block, then assign the members of block 1 to a weight-loss treatment, then assign block 2, etc. For example, starting on line 133, we assign 4-Moses to treatment A, 1-Williams to B, and 3-Hernandez to C (so that 2-Deng gets treatment D), then carry on for block 2, etc. (either continuing on the same line, or starting over somewhere else).

5.41 (a)

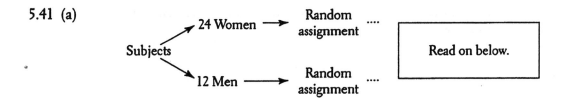

Following the "random assignment," the top branch of the diagram splits into six groups of 4 women each, and the bottom splits into six groups with 2 men in each. Each group receives the appropriate treatment (1–6), and then the subjects' attitudes about the product, etc., are measured. (b) Number the women from 01 to 24, and the men from 01 to 12. First we look for 20 women's numbers, and find: 12, 13, 04, 18, 19, 24, 23, 16, 02, 08, 17, 21, 10, 05, 09, 06, 01, 20, 22, and 07. Continuing on to find 10 men's numbers, we get 05, 09, 07, 02, 01, 08, 11, 06, 12, and 04. Then, for example, Women's Group 1 will be the first four women selected, namely 12, 13, 04, and 18. This gives us the following layout:

Women									Men			
01	5	07	5	13	1	19	2		01	3	07	2
02	3	08	3	14	6	20	5		02	2	08	3
03	6	09	4	15	6	21	3		03	6	09	1
04	1	10	4	16	2	22	5		04	5	10	6
05	4	11	6	17	3	23	2		05	1	11	4
06	4	12	1	18	1	24	2		06	4	12	5

5.42 For each person, randomly decide which hand they should use first — either by flipping a coin (heads: right hand first, tails: left hand first) or by taking digits from Table B (even: right, odd: left).

5.43 The randomization will vary with the starting line in Table B. *Completely randomized design:* Randomly assign 10 students to "Group 1" (which has the trend-highlighting software) and the other 10 to "Group 2" (which does not). Compare the performance of Group 1 with that of Group 2. *Matched pairs design:* Each student does the activity twice, once with the software and once without. Randomly decide (for each student) whether they have the software the first or second time. Compare performance with the software and without it. (This randomization can be done by flipping a coin 20 times, or by picking 20 digits from Table B, and using the software first if the digit is even, etc.) *Alternate matched pairs design:* Again, all students do the activity twice. Randomly assign 10 students to Group 1 and 10 to Group 2. Group 1 uses the software the first time; Group 2 uses the software the second time.

5.44 (a) Assign 10 subjects to Group 1 (the 70° group) and the other 10 to Group 2 (which will perform the task in the 90° condition). Record the number of correct insertions in each group. (b) All subjects will perform the task twice — once in each temperature condition. Randomly choose which temperature each subject works in first, either by flipping a coin, or by placing 10 subjects in Group 1 (70°, then 90°) and the other 10 in Group 2.

5.45 (a) It is an experiment (albeit a poorly designed one) because a treatment (herbal tea) is imposed on the subjects. (b) No, it is a study — the scores on the English test are merely observed for the various subjects.

5.46 (a) The subjects are the 210 children. (b) The factor is the "choice set"; there are three levels (2 milk/2 fruit drink, 4 milk/2 fruit drink, and 2 milk/4 fruit drink). (c) The response variable is the choice made by each child.

5.47 (a) The subjects are the physicians, the factor is medication (with two levels — aspirin and placebo), and the response is observing health, specifically whether the subjects have heart attacks or not.

(b)

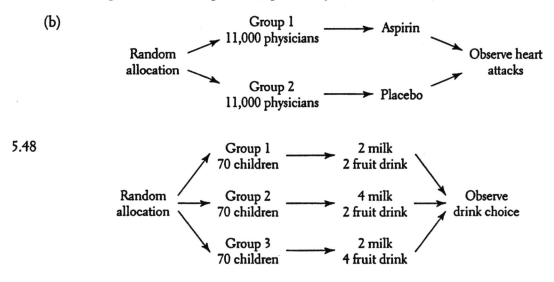

5.48

5.49 (a) Randomly assign 20 men to each of two groups. Record each subject's blood pressure, then apply the treatments: a calcium supplement for Group 1, and a placebo for Group 2. After sufficient time has passed, measure blood pressure again and observe any change. (b) Number from 01 to 40 down the columns. Group 1 is 18-Howard, 20-Imrani, 26-Maldonado, 35-Tompkins, 39-Willis, 16-Guillen, 04-Bikalis, 21-James, 19-Hruska, 37-Tullock, 29-O'Brian, 07-Cranston, 34-Solomon, 22-Kaplan, 10-Durr, 25-Liang, 13-Fratianna, 38-Underwood, 15-Green, and 05-Chen.

5.50 Label the children from 001 to 210, then consider three digits at a time. The first five children in Group 1 are numbers 119, 033, 199, 192, and 148.

5.51 Responding to a placebo does not imply that the complaint was not "real" — 38% of the placebo group in the gastric freezing experiment improved, and those patients really had ulcers. The placebo effect is a *psychological* response, but it may make an actual *physical* improvement in the patient's health.

5.52 (a) Each subject takes both tests; the order in which the tests are taken is randomly chosen. (b) Take 22 digits from Table B. If the first digit is even, subject 1 takes the BI first; if it is odd, he or she takes the ARSMA first. (Or, administer the BI first if the first digit is 0–4, and the ARSMA first if it is 5–9.)

5.53 (a)

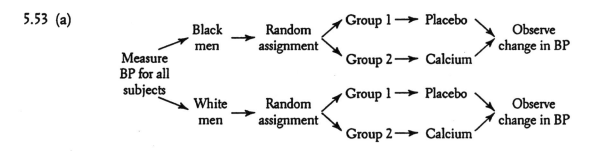

(b) A larger group gives more information — when more subjects are involved, the random differences between individuals have less influence, and we can expect the average of our sample to be a better representation of the whole population.

SECTION 5.3

5.54 The choice of digits in these simulations may of course vary from that made here. In (a)–(c), a single digit simulates the response; for (d), two digits simulate the response of a single voter.

(a) Odd digits   — voter would vote Democratic
Even digits   — voter would vote for Republican

(b) 0, 1, 2, 3, 4, 5 — Democratic
6, 7, 8, 9   — Republican

(c) 0, 1, 2, 3   — Democratic
4, 5, 6, 7   — Republican
8, 9   — Undecided

(d) 00, 01, ..., 52 — Democratic
53, 54, ..., 99 — Republican

5.55 For the choices made in the solution to Exercise 5.54,

(a) D, R, R, R, R, R, D, R, D — 3 Democrats, 7 Republicans
(b) R, D, D, R, R, R, R, D, R, R — 3 Democrats, 7 Republicans
(c) R, U, R, D, R, U, U, U, D, R — 2 Democrats, 4 Republicans, 4 undecided
(d) R, R, R, D, D, D, D, D, D, R — 6 Democrats, 4 Republicans

5.56 (a) Obtain an alphabetized list of the student body, and assign consecutive numbers to the students on the list. Use a random process to select 10 students from this list. (b) Let the digits 0 to 7 represent a student who would answer "Yes" that they favor abolishing evening exams, and let the digits 8 and 9 represent those students who would answer "No." (c) The first 10 students selected are represented by: 3 6 7 5 9 5 8 9 8 4. The numbers underlined represent "Yes" answers, for 60%. In the 25 repetitions, only the 9th, 18th, and 23rd resulted in all 10 simulated students answering "Yes," for 12%. (Theoretically, all 10 would respond "Yes" approximately 10.7% of the time, so our simulation results are quite reasonable.)

5.57 (a) A single random digit simulates one shot, with 0 to 6 a hit and 7, 8, or 9 a miss. Then 5 consecutive digits simulate 5 independent shots.

(b) Let 0–6 < "hit" and 7, 8, 9 > "miss." Starting with line 125, the first four repetitions are:

9 6 7 4 6   1 2 1 4 9   3 7 8 2 3   7 1 8 6 8
   (3)   (4)   (3)   (2)

Each block of 5 digits in the table represents one repetition of the 5 attempted free throws. The underlined digits represent hits. We perform 46 more repetitions for a total of 50, and calculate the proportion of times the player makes 2 or fewer shots. Here are the number of hits for the 50 repetitions.

3 4 3 2 4   4 5 4 2 3   3 3 2 2 3   4 3 1 5 4
4 4 3 4 3   4 5 4 5 3   2 2 3 2 2   4 3 5 3 2
4 3 2 3 4   3 3 3 4 5

The frequency counts are

X	0	1	2	3	4	5
Freq.	0	1	10	18	15	6

The relative frequency of 2 or fewer hits in 5 attempts is 11/50 = .22.

   Note: It will be shown in Chapter 8 that the theoretical probability of missing 3 or more shots (i.e., making 2 or fewer shots) is 0.1631, or about one time in six.

5.58 (a) Change randInt(0, 9, 5) to randInt(0, 99, 5) and change sum($L_1 \geq 7$ and $L_1 \leq 9$) to sum($L_1 \geq 78$ and $L_1 \leq 99$). (b) For 25 repetitions: Rel. Freq. = .12; for 50 repetitions: Rel. Freq. = .14; for 100 repetitions: Rel. Freq. = .14.

5.59 Let 1 = girl and 0 = boy. The command randInt(0, 1) produces a 0 or 1 with equal likelihood. Continue to press ENTER. In 50 repetitions, we got a girl 47 times, and all 4 boys three times. Our simulation produced a girl 94% of the time, vs. a theoretical probability of 0.938.

5.60 (a) Let 000 to 999 ↔ a bats, 000 to 319 ↔ hits, and 320 to 999 ↔ no hits.

   (b) We entered 1 → c ENTER to set a counter. Then enter
randInt (0, 999, 20) → L_1 : sum ($L_1 \geq 0$ and $L_1 \leq 319$) → L_2 (C) : C + 1 > C and press ENTER repeatedly. The count (number of the repetition) is displayed on the screen to help you see when to stop. The results for the 20 repetitions are stored in list L_2. We obtained the following frequencies:

Number of hits in 20 at bats	4	5	6	7	8	9
Frequency	3	5	4	3	2	3

   (c) The mean number of hits in 20 at bats was $\bar{x}$ = 6.25. And 6.25/20 = .3125, compared with the player's batting average of .320. Notice that even though there was considerable variability in the 20 repetitions, ranging from a low of 3 hits to a high of 9 hits, the results of our simulation were very close to the player's batting average.

5.61 The command randInt(1, 365, 23) → L_1 : SortA (L_1) randomly selects 23 birthdays and assigns them to L_1. Then it sorts the day in increasing order. Scroll through the list to see duplicate birthdays. Repeat many times. For a large number of repetitions, there should be duplicate birthdays about half the time. To simulate 41 people, change 23 to 41 in the command and repeat many times. We assume that there are 365 days for birthdays, and that all days are equally likely to be a birthday.

5.62 This simulation is fun for students, but the record-keeping can be challenging! Here is one method. First number the (real or imaginary) participants 1–25. Write the numbers 1–25 on the board so that you can strike through them as they hear the rumor. We used randInt(1, 25) to randomly select a person to begin spreading the rumor, and then pressed ENTER repeatedly to randomly select additional people to hear the rumor. We made a table to record the round (time increment), those who knew the rumor and were spreading it, those randomly selected to hear the rumor, and those who stopped spreading it because the person randomly selected to hear it had already heard it. Here is the beginning of our simulation, to illustrate our scheme:

Time incr	Knows	Tells	Stopped
1	16 →	2	
2	2 →	25	
	16 →	3	
3	2	19	
	3	6	
	16	15	
	25	1	
4	1	21	
	2	5	
	3	23	
	6	13	
	15	25	15
	16	9	
	19	16	19
	25	15	25
5			

Eventually we crossed off all but 7, 12, 14, and 24, so 4 out of 25 or 4/25 = 16% never heard the rumor. It can be shown that with a sufficiently large population, approximately 20% of the population will not hear the rumor.

5.63 (a) Read two random digits at a time from Table B. Let 01 to 13 represent a Heart, let 14 to 52 represent another suit, and ignore the other two-digit numbers. (b) You should beat Slim about 44% of the time.

5.64 We started a counter (C), and then executed the command shown, pressing the ENTER key 30 times for 30 repetitions.

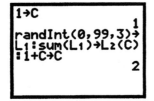 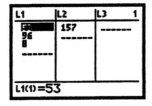

For five sets of 30 repetitions, we observed 5, 3, 3, 8, and 4 numbers that were multiples of 5. The mean number of multiples of 5 in 30 repetitions was 3.6, so 3.6/30 = 12% is our estimate for the proportion of times a person wins the game.

5.65 (a) One digit simulates system A's response: 0 to 8 shut down the reactor, and 9 fails to shut it down. (b) One digit simulates system B's response: 0 to 7 shut down the reactor, and 8 or 9 fail. (c) A pair of consecutive digits simulates the response of both systems, the first giving A's response as in (a), and the second B's response as in (b). If a single digit were used to simulate both systems, the reactions of A and B would be dependent — for example, if A fails, then B must also fail. (d) The true probability that the reactor will shut down is $1 - (0.2)(0.1) = 0.98$.

CHAPTER REVIEW

5.66 (a) The population is Ontario residents; the sample is the 61,239 people interviewed. (b) The sample size is very large, so if there were large numbers of both sexes in the sample — this is a safe assumption since we are told this is a "random sample" — these two numbers should be fairly accurate reflections of the values for the whole population.

5.67 (a) Explanatory variable: treatment method; response: survival times. (b) No treatment is actively imposed; the women (or their doctors) chose which treatment to use. (c) Doctors may make the decision of which treatment to recommend based in part on how advanced the case is. Some might be more likely to recommend the older treatment for advanced cases, in which case the chance of recovery is lower. Other doctors might view the older treatment as not being worth the effort, and recommend the newer method as a way of providing *some* hope for recovery while minimizing the trauma and expense of major surgery.

5.68 No, it is a study — no treatment is imposed; the researchers simply measure the fitness of the executives.

5.69 (a) Label the students from 0001 to 3478. (b) Taking four digits at a time gives 2940, 0769, 1481, 2975, and 1315.

5.70 A stratified random sample would be useful here; one could select 50 faculty members from each level. Alternatively, select 25 (or 50) institutions of each size, then choose 2 (or 1) faculty members at each institution.

    If a large proportion of faculty in your state work at a particular class of institution, it may be useful to stratify unevenly. If, for example, about 50% teach at Class I institutions, you may want half your sample to come from Class I institutions.

5.71 (a) One possible population: all full-time undergraduate students in the fall term on a list provided by the Registrar. (b) A stratified sample with 125 students from each year is one possibility. (c) Mailed questionnaires might have high nonresponse rates. Telephone interviews exclude those without phones, and may mean repeated calling for those that are not home. Face-to-face interviews might be more costly than your funding will allow.

5.72 (a) The chicks are the experimental units; weight gain is the response variable. (b) There are two factors: corn variety (2 levels) and percent of protein (3 levels). This makes 6 treatments, so 60 chicks are required.

| | | Factor B: Protein level | | |
		12%	16%	20%
Factor A:	opaque-2	1	2	3
Corn variety	floury-2	4	5	6

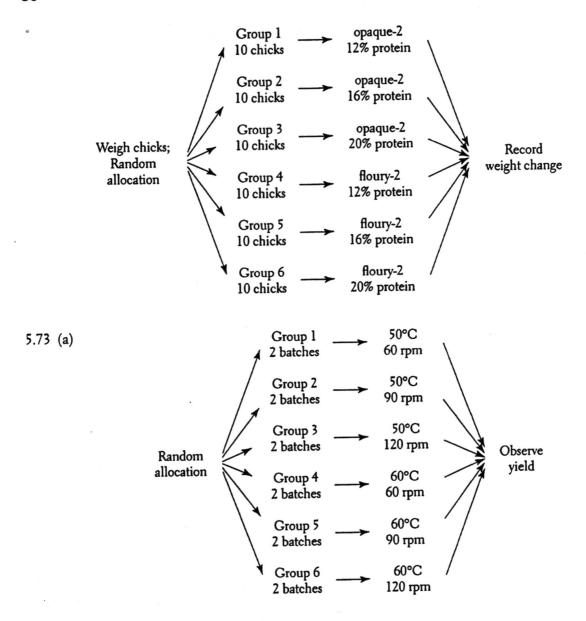

5.73 (a)

(b) The first 10 numbers (between 01 and 12) are 06, 09, 03, 05, 04, 07, 02, 08, 10, and 11. So the 6th and 9th batches will receive treatment 1; batches 3 and 5 will be processed with treatment 2, etc.

5.74 The factors are whether or not the letter has a ZIP code (2 levels: yes or no), and the time of day the letter is mailed. The number of levels for the second factor may vary.

To deal with lurking variables, all letters should be the same size and should be sent to the same city, and the day on which a letter is sent should be randomly selected. Because most post offices have shorter hours on Saturdays, one may wish to give that day some sort of "special treatment" (it might even be a good idea to have the day of the week be a *third* factor in this experiment).

5.75 Each subject should taste both kinds of cheeseburger, in a randomly selected order, and then be asked about their preference. Both burgers should have the same "fixings" (ketchup, mustard, etc.). Since some subjects might be able to identify the cheeseburgers by appearance, one might need to take additional steps (such as blindfolding, or serving only the center part of the burger) in order to make this a true "blind" experiment.

5.77 It means that the correlation is large enough (presumably, though not necessarily, in the positive direction) that it is unlikely to have occurred just by chance.

5.78 (a) A single run: spin the 1–10 spinner twice; see if the larger of the two numbers is larger than 5. The player wins if either number is 6, 7, 8, 9, or 10. (b) If using the random digit table, let 0 represent 10, and let the digits 1–9 represent themselves. (c) randInt(1, 10, 2). (d) In our simulation of 20 repetitions, we observed 13 wins for a 65% win rate. Using the methods of the next chapter, it can be shown that there is a 75% probability of winning this game.

5.79 (a) Let 01 to 05 represent demand for 0 cheesecakes
Let 06 to 20 represent demand for 1 cheesecake
Let 21 to 45 represent demand for 2 cheesecakes
Let 46 to 70 represent demand for 3 cheesecakes
Let 71 to 90 represent demand for 4 cheesecakes
Let 91 to 99 and 00 represent demand for 5 cheesecakes

(b) Our results suggest that the baker should make 2 cheesecakes each day to maximize his profits.

5.80 Since Carla makes 80% of her free throws, let a single digit represent a free throw, and let $0–7 \leftrightarrow$ "hit" and $8, 9 \leftrightarrow$ "miss." We instructed the calculator to simulate a free throw, and store the result in L_1. Then we instructed the calculator to see if the attempt was a hit (1) or a miss (0), and record that fact in L_2. Continue to press ENTER until there are 20 simulated free throws.

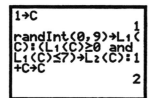 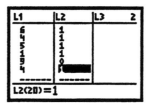

Scroll through L_2 and determine the longest string of 1's (consecutive baskets). In our first set of 20 repetitions, we observed 8 consecutive baskets. Additional sets of 20 repetitions produced: 11, 9, 9, and 8. The average longest run was 9 consecutive baskets in 20 attempts. The five number summary: Min = 8, Q_1 = 8, Med = 9, Q_3 = 10, and Max = 11. There was surprising little variation in our five groups of 20 repetitions.

5.81 (a) A single digit simulates one try, with 0 or 1 a pass and 2 to 9 a failure. Three independent tries are simulated by three successive random digits. (b) With the convention of (a), 50 tries beginning in line 120 gives 25 successes, so the probability of success is estimated as 25/50 = 1/2. [In doing the simulation, remember that you can end a repetition after 1 or 2 tries if the student passes, so that some repetitions do not use three digits. Though this is a proper simulation of the student's behavior, the probability of at least one pass is the same if three digits are examined in every repetition. The true probability is $1 - (0.8)^3 = 0.488$, so this particular simulation was quite accurate.] (c) No—learning usually occurs in taking an exam, so the probability of passing probably increases on each trial.

5.82 (a) The three tries are simulated by three consecutive random digits (stopping after a pass); 0 and 1 are a pass on the first try, 0, 1, and 2 a pass on the second try, and 0, 1, 2, and 3 a pass on the third try. (b) The correct probability is $1 - (0.8)(0.7)(0.6) = 0.664$. Taking groups of three digits at a time (not quitting early after a pass) gives 36 passes, so the estimated probability is 0.72. If one does quit early after a pass, there are 32 passes, so the estimated probability is 0.64.

6

Probability: The Study of Randomness

SECTION 6.1

6.1 Long trials of this experiment often approach 40% heads. One theory attributes this surprising result to a "bottle-cap effect" due to an unequal rim on the penny.

6.2 Answers will vary depending on the size of the paper clip.

6.3 Results will vary with the type of thumbtack used.

6.4 Answers will vary.

6.5 In the long run, of a large number of hands of five cards, about 2% (one out of 50) will contain a three of a kind. [*Note:* This probability is actually $88/4165 \approx 0.02113$.]

6.6 The theoretical probabilities are, in order: 1/16, 4/16 = 1/4, 6/16 = 3/8, 4/16 = 1/4, 1/16.

6.7 (b) In our simulation, Shak hit 52% of his shots. (c) The longest sequence of misses in our run was 6 and the longest sequence of hits was 9. Of course, results will vary.

6.8 (a) 0. (b) 1. (c) 0.01. (d) 0.6 (or 0.99, but "more often than not" is a rather weak description of an event with probability 0.99!)

SECTION 6.2

6.9 (a) S = {germinates, does not germinate}. (b) If measured in weeks, for example, S = {0, 1, 2, . . . }. (c) S = {A, B, C, D, F}. (d) S = {misses both, makes one, makes both}, or S = {misses both, makes first/misses second, misses first/makes second, makes both}. (e) S = {1, 2, 3, 4, 5, 6, 7}.

6.10 (a) S = {all numbers between 0 and 24}. (b) S = {0, 1, 2, ... 11000}. (c) S = {0, 1, 2, . . . , 12}. (d) S = {all numbers greater than or equal to 0}, or S = {0, 0.01, 0.02, 0.03, . . . }. (e) S = {all positive and negative numbers}. Note that the rats can lose weight.

6.11 S = {all numbers between ____ and ____}. The numbers in the blanks may vary. Table 1.8 has values from 86 to 195 cal; the range of values in S should include *at least* those numbers. Some students may play it safe and say "all numbers greater than 0."

6.12 If two coins are tossed, then by the multiplication principle, there are (2) (2) = 4 possible outcomes. The outcomes are illustrated in the following tree diagram:

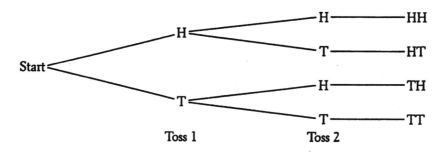

Toss 1   Toss 2

The sample space is {HH, HT, TH, TT}. (b) If three coins are tossed, then there are (2) (2) (2) = 8 possible outcomes. The outcomes are illustrated in the following tree diagram:

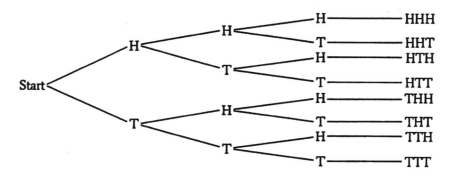

The sample space is {HHH, HHT, HTH, HTT, THH, THT, TTH, TTT}. (c) If four coins are tossed, then there are (2) (2) (2) (2) = 16 possible outcomes, each of which consists of a string of four letters that may be H's or T's. The sample space is {HHHH, HHHT, HHTH, HTHH,THHH, HHTT, HTHT, HTTH, THTH, TTHH, THHT, HTTT, THTT, TTHT, TTTH, TTTT}.

6.13 (a) 10 × 10 × 10 × 10 = 10^4 = 10,000. (b) 10 × 9 × 8 × 7 = 5,040. (c) There are 10,000 four-digit tags, 1,000 three-digit tags, 100 two-digit tags, and 10 one-digit tags, for a total of 11,110 license tags.

6.14 (a) An outcome of this experiment consists of a string of 3 digits, each of which can be 1,2, or 3. By the multiplication principle, the number of possible outcomes is (3) (3) (3) = 27. (b) The sample space is {111, 112, 113, 121, 122, 123, 131, 132, 133, 211, 212, 213, 221, 222, 223, 231, 232, 233, 311, 312, 313, 321, 322, 323, 331, 332, 333}.

6.15 (a) 10 × 10 × 10 ((seal)) × 10 × 10 × 10 = 10^6 = 1,000,000. (b) 26 × 26 × 26 × 10 × 10 × 10 ■ 17,576,000. (c) 17,576,000 × 10 = 175,760,000.

6.16 (a) For each new exchange, there are (10) (10) (10) (10) = 10,000 additional telephone numbers, since each of the remaining digits can be any of the digits 0, 1, 12, . . . , 9. (b) For each new area code, there are (8) (10) (10) (10) (10) (10) (10) = 8,000,000 additional phone numbers, since the first digit of the seven-digit number cannot be 0 or 1 and the remaining six digits can be any of the digits 0, 1, . . . 9.

6.17 There are 19 outcomes where at least one digit occurs in the correct position: 111, 112, 113, 121, 122, 123, 131, 132, 133, 213, 221, 222, 223, 233, 313, 321, 322, 323, 333. The theoretical probability of at least one digit occurring in the correct position is therefore 19/27 = .7037.

6.18 (a) The given probabilities have sum 0.96, so P(type AB) = 0.04. (b) P(type O or B) = 0.49 + 0.20 = 0.69.

6.19 (a) The sum of the given probabilities is 0.9, so $P(\text{blue}) = 0.1$. (b) The sum of the given probabilities is 0.7, so $P(\text{blue}) = 0.3$. (c) $P(\text{plain M\&M is red, yellow, or orange}) = 0.2 + 0.2 + 0.1 = 0.5$. $P(\text{peanut M\&M is red, yellow, or orange}) = 0.1 + 0.2 + 0.1 = 0.4$.

6.20 Use the complement rule: $1 - 0.46 = 0.54$.

6.21 $P(\text{either CV disease or cancer}) = 0.45 + 0.22 = 0.67$; $P(\text{other cause}) = 1 - 0.67 = 0.33$.

6.22 (a) $P(\text{not forested}) = 1 - 0.35 = 0.65$. (b) $P(\text{forest or pasture}) = 0.35 + 0.03 = 0.38$. (c) $P(\text{neither forest nor pasture}) = 1 - 0.38 = 0.62$.

6.23 (a) The sum is 1, as we expect since all possible outcomes are listed. (b) $1 - 0.41 = 0.59$. (c) $0.41 + 0.23 = 0.64$. (d) $(0.41)(0.41) = 0.1681$.

6.24 Fight one big battle: His probability of winning is 0.6, compared to $0.8^3 = 0.512$. (Or he could choose to try for a negotiated peace.)

6.25 $(1 - 0.05)^{12} = (0.95)^{12} = 0.5404$.

6.26 No: It is unlikely that these events are independent. In particular, it is reasonable to expect that college graduates are less likely to be laborers or operators.

6.27 (a) $P(A) = \frac{38,225}{166,438} = 0.230$ since there are 38,225 (thousand) people who have completed 4+ years of college out of 166,438 (thousand). (b) $P(B) = \frac{52,022}{166,438} = 0.313$. (c) $P(A \text{ and } B) = \frac{8,005}{166,438} = 0.048$; A and B are not independent since $P(A \text{ and } B) \neq P(A)P(B)$.

6.28 Model 1: Legitimate. Model 2: Legitimate. Model 3: Probabilities have sum $\frac{6}{7}$. Model 4: Probabilities cannot be negative.

6.29 (a) Legitimate. (b) Not legitimate, because probabilities sum to more than 1. (c) Not legitimate, because probabilities sum to less than 1.

6.30 (a) $P(A) = 0.09 + 0.20 = 0.29$. $P(B) = 0.09 + 0.05 + 0.04 = 0.18$. (b) A^c is the event that the farm is 50 or more acres in size; $P(A^c) = 1 - 0.29 = 0.71$. (c) $\{A \text{ or } B\}$ is the event that a farm is either less than 50 or more than 500 acres in size; $P(A \text{ or } B) = 0.29 + 0.18 = 0.47$.

6.31 (a) The probabilities sum to 1. (b) Adding up the second row gives $P(\text{female}) = 0.43$. (c) $1 - 0.03 - 0.01 = 0.96$. (d) $0.11 + 0.12 + 0.01 + 0.04 = 0.28$. (e) $1 - 0.28 = 0.72$.

6.32 (a) 1/38. (b) Since 18 slots are red, the probability of a red is $P(\text{red}) = \frac{18}{38} = 0.474$. (c) There are 12 winning slots, so $P(\text{win a column bet}) = \frac{12}{38} = 0.316$.

6.33 Look at the first five rolls in each sequence. All have one G and four R's, so those probabilities are the same. In the first sequence, you win regardless of the sixth roll; for the second, you win if the sixth roll is G, and for the third sequence, you win if it is R. The respective probabilities are $(\frac{2}{6})^4 (\frac{4}{6}) = \frac{2}{243} = 0.00823$, $(\frac{2}{6})^4 (\frac{4}{6})^2 = \frac{4}{729} = 0.00549$, and $(\frac{2}{6})^5 (\frac{4}{6}) = \frac{2}{729} = 0.00274$.

6.34 $P(\text{first child is albino}) = \frac{1}{2} \times \frac{1}{2} = \frac{1}{4}$. $P(\text{both of two children are albino}) = \frac{1}{4} \times \frac{1}{4} = \frac{1}{16}$. $P(\text{neither is albino}) = (1 - \frac{1}{4})^2 = \frac{9}{16}$.

6.35 (a) $(0.65)^3 = 0.2746$ (under the random walk theory). (b) 0.35 (since performance in separate years is independent). (c) $(0.65)^2 + (0.35)^2 = 0.545$.

6.36 (a) $P(\text{under 65}) = 0.321 + 0.124 = 0.445$. $P(\text{65 or older}) = 1 - 0.445 = 0.555$. (b) $P(\text{tests done}) = 0.321 + 0.365 = 0.686$. $P(\text{tests not done}) = 1 - 0.686 = 0.314$. (c) $P(A \text{ and } B) = 0.365$; $P(A)P(B) = (0.555)(0.686) = 0.3807$. A and B are not independent; tests were done less frequently on older patients than if these events were independent.

SECTION 6.3

6.37 $P(A \text{ or } B) = P(A) + P(B) - P(A \text{ and } B) = 0.125 + 0.237 - 0.077 = 0.285.$

6.38 $P(A \text{ or } B) = P(A) + P(B) - P(A \text{ and } B) = 0.6 + 0.4 - 0.2 = 0.8.$

6.39 (a) {A and B}: household is both prosperous and educated; $P(A \text{ and } B) = 0.077$ (given). (b) {A and B^c}: household is prosperous but not educated; $P(A \text{ and } B^c) = P(A) - P(A \text{ and } B) = 0.048.$ (c) {A^c and B}: household is not prosperous but is educated; $P(A^c \text{ and } B) = P(B) - P(A \text{ and } B) = 0.160.$ (d) {A^c and B^c}: household is neither prosperous nor educated; $P(A^c \text{ and } B^c) = 0.715$ (so that the probabilities add to 1).

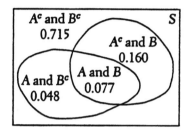

6.40 (a) This event is {A and B}; $P(A \text{ and } B) = 0.2$ (given). (b) This is {A and B^c}; $P(A \text{ and } B^c) = P(A) - P(A \text{ and } B) = 0.4.$ (c) This is {A^c and B}; $P(A^c \text{ and } B) = P(B) - P(A \text{ and } B) = 0.2.$ (d) This is {A^c and B^c}; $P(A^c \text{ and } B^c) = 0.2$ (so that the probabilities add to 1).

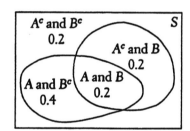

6.41 (a) $\frac{18,262}{99,585} = 0.1834.$ (b) $\frac{7,767}{18,262} = 0.4253.$ (c) $\frac{7,767}{99,585} = 0.0780.$ (d) $P(\text{over 65 and married}) = P(\text{over 65}) P(\text{married} \mid \text{over 65}) = (0.1834)(0.4253).$ (Or, look at the fractions and notice the cancellation when we multiply.)

6.42 (a) $\frac{11,080}{99,585} = 0.1113.$ (b) $\frac{8,636}{18,262} = 0.4729.$ (c) $\frac{2,425}{68,709} = 0.0353.$ (d) No: Among other reasons, if they were independent, the answers to (a) and (b) would be the same. (We would hardly expect them to be independent.)

6.43 (a) $\frac{3,016}{58,929} = 0.0517.$ (b) "0.241 is the proportion of women who are *married* among those women who are *age 18 to 24*." (c) "0.0517 is the proportion of women who are *age 18 to 24* among those women who are *married*."

6.44 (a) $\frac{856}{1,626} = 0.5264.$ (b) $\frac{30}{74} = 0.4054.$ (c) No: If they were independent, the answers to (a) and (b) would be the same.

6.45 (a) $\frac{770}{1,626} = 0.4736.$ (b) $\frac{529}{770} = 0.6870.$ (c) Using the multiplication rule: $P(\text{male and bachelor's degree}) = P(\text{male}) P(\text{bachelor's degree} \mid \text{male}) = (0.4736)(0.6870) = 0.3254.$ (Answers will vary with how much previous answers had been rounded.) Directly: $\frac{529}{1,626} = 0.3253.$ [Note that the difference between these answers is inconsequential, since the numbers in the table are rounded to the nearest thousand anyway.]

6.46 There were $24,457 + 6,027 = 30,484$ suicides altogether. (a) $\frac{24,457}{30,484} = 0.8023.$ (b) $\frac{15,802 + 2,367}{30,484} = 0.5960.$ (c) Among men: $\frac{15,802}{24,457} = 0.6461.$ Among women: $\frac{2,367}{6,027} = 0.3927.$ (d) In choosing a suicide method, men are much more likely than women to use a firearm.

6.47 In constructing the Venn diagram, start with the numbers given for "only tea" and "all three," then determine other values. For example, P (coffee and cola, but not tea) $= P$ (coffee and cola) $- P$ (all three). (a) 15% drink only cola. (b) 20% drink none of these.

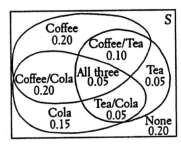

6.48 $P(A \text{ and } B) = P(A) P(B \mid A) = 0.1472.$

6.49 If $F = \{\text{dollar falls}\}$ and $R = \{\text{renegotiation demanded}\}$, then $P(F \text{ and } R) = P(F) P(R \mid F) = (0.4)(0.8) = 0.32.$

6.50 (a) $P(A) = 0.846$, $P(B \mid A) = 0.951$, $P(B \mid A^c) = 0.919.$ (b) On right. (c) $P(A \text{ and } B) = (0.846)(0.951) = 0.8045.$ $P(A^c \text{ and } B) = (0.154)(0.919) = 0.1415.$ $P(B) = 0.8045 + 0.1415 = 0.9460.$

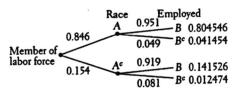

6.51 If $F = \{\text{dollar falls}\}$ and $R = \{\text{renegotiation demanded}\}$, then $P(R) = P(F \text{ and } R) + P(F^c \text{ and } R) = 0.32 + P(F^c) P(R \mid F^c) = 0.32 + (0.6)(0.2) = 0.44.$

6.52 $P(A \mid B) = \dfrac{P(A \text{ and } B)}{P(B)} = \dfrac{0.8045}{0.9460} = 0.8504.$

6.53 $P(\text{correct}) = P(\text{knows answer}) + P(\text{doesn't know, but guesses correctly}) = 0.75 + (0.25)(0.20) = 0.8.$

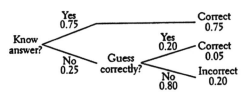

6.54 Tree diagram on right. The black candidate expects to get $12\% + 36\% + 10\% = 58\%$ of the vote.

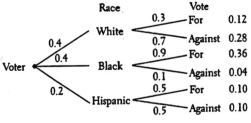

6.55 $P(\text{knows the answer} \mid \text{gives the correct answer}) = \frac{0.75}{0.80} = \frac{15}{16} = 0.9375.$

6.56 The event $\{Y < 1/2\}$ is the bottom half of the square, while $\{Y > X\}$ is the upper left triangle of the square. They overlap in a triangle with area 1/8, so

$$P(Y < \tfrac{1}{2} \mid Y > X) = \frac{P(Y < \tfrac{1}{2} \text{ and } Y > X)}{P(Y > X)} = \frac{1/8}{1/2} = \frac{1}{4}.$$

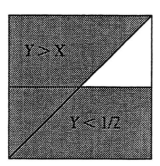

CHAPTER REVIEW

6.57 The fraction: (points in quarter disk)/(points in square) ≈ (area of quarter disk)/(area of square) = $(\pi (1)/4)/(1)$, so $\pi \approx$ (the proportion of points in the disk) × 4.

6.58 In the diagram below, the shaded square has side with length 2 and is centered at the center of the larger square. By geometry, if the *center* of the disk (which lands at random on the grid by assumption) lands anywhere *inside the shaded square*, then the disk will lie entirely within the large square.

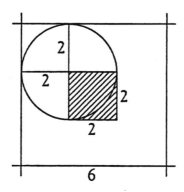

Thus, the theoretical probability of winning is: (area of shaded square)/(area of large square) = 4/36 = 1/9. Thus, as is usually the case with carnival games, a player's chances of winning the stuffed animal are not very good.

6.59 (a) There are 10 pairs. Just using initials: {(A,D), (A,J), (A,S), (A,R), (D,J), (D,S), (D,R), (J,S), (J,R), (S,R)} (b) Each has probability 1/10 = 10%. (c) Julie is chosen in 4 of the 10 possible outcomes: 4/10 = 40%. (d) There are 3 pairs with neither Sam nor Roberto, so the probability is 3/10.

6.60 $(1 - 0.02)^{20} = (0.98)^{20} = 0.6676.$

6.61 (a) $P(\text{B or O}) = 0.13 + 0.44 = 0.57$. (b) $P(\text{wife has type B and husband has type A}) = (0.13)(0.37) = 0.0481$. (c) $P(\text{one has type A and other has type B}) = (0.13)(0.37) + (0.37)(0.13) = 0.0962$. (d) $P(\text{at least one has type O}) = 1 - P(\text{neither has type O}) = 1 - (1 - 0.44)(1 - 0.44) = 0.6864$.

6.62 (a) $P(\text{female} \mid A) = \frac{0.09}{0.14 + 0.09} = \frac{9}{23} = 0.3913$.

(b) $P(\text{female} \mid D \text{ or } E) = \frac{0.01 + 0.04}{0.11 + 0.12 + 0.01 + 0.04} = \frac{5}{28} = 0.1786$.

6.63 (a) $P(X \geq 50) = 0.14 + 0.05 = 0.19$. (b) $P(X \geq 100 \mid X \geq 50) = \frac{0.05}{0.19} = \frac{5}{19}$.

6.64 If $I = \{\text{infection}\}$ and $F = \{\text{failure}\}$, then $P(I \text{ or } F) = P(I) + P(F) - P(I \text{ and } F) = 0.03 + 0.14 - 0.01 = 0.16$. The requested probability is $P(I^c \text{ and } F^c) = 1 - P(I \text{ or } F) = 0.84$.

6.65 The response will be "no" with probability $0.35 = (0.5)(0.7)$. If the probability of plagiarism were 0.2, then $P(\text{student answers "no"}) = 0.4 = (0.05)(0.8)$. If 39% of students surveyed answered "no," then we estimate that $2 \times 39\% = 78\%$ have *not* plagiarized, so about 22% have plagiarized.

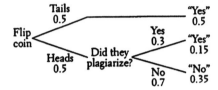

6.66 (a) On right. (b) $P(\text{positive}) = 0.01485 + 0.00997 = 0.02482$. (c) $P(\text{has antibody} \mid \text{positive}) = \frac{0.00997}{0.02482} = 0.4017$.

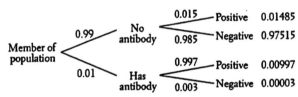

Random Variables

7

SECTION 7.1

7.1 $P(\text{less than } 3) = P(1 \text{ or } 2) = \frac{2}{6} = \frac{1}{3}$.

7.2 (a) BBB, BBG, BGB, GBB, GGB, GBG, BGG, GGG. Each has probability 1/8. (b) Three of the eight arrangements have two (and only two) girls, so $P(X = 2) = 3/8 = 0.375$. (c) See table.

Value of X	0	1	2	3
Probability	1/8	3/8	3/8	1/8

7.3 (a) 1%. (b) All probabilities are between 0 and 1; the probabilities add to 1. (c) $P(X \leq 3) = 0.48 + 0.38 + 0.08 = 1 - 0.01 - 0.05 = 0.94$. (d) $P(X < 3) = 0.48 + 0.38 = 0.86$. (e) Write either $X \geq 4$ or $X > 3$. The probability is $0.05 + 0.01 = 0.06$. (f) Read two random digits from Table B. Here is the correspondence: 01 to 48 ↔ Class 1, 49 to 86 ↔ Class 2, 87 to 94 ↔ Class 3, 95 to 99 ↔ Class 4, and 00 ↔ Class 5. Repeatedly generate 2 digit random numbers. The proportion of numbers in the range 01 to 94 will be an estimate of the required probability.

7.4 (a) $P(0 \leq X \leq 0.4) = 0.4$. (b) $P(0.4 \leq X \leq 1) = 0.6$. (c) $P(0.3 \leq X \leq 0.5) = 0.2$. (d) $P(0.3 < X < 0.5) = 0.2$. (e) $P(0.226 \leq X \leq 0.713) = 0.713 - 0.226 = 0.487$.

7.5 (a) $P(X \leq 0.49) = 0.49$. (b) $P(X \geq 0.27) = 0.73$. (c) $P(0.27 < X < 1.27) = P(0.27 < X < 1) = 0.73$. (d) $P(0.1 \leq X \leq 0.2 \text{ or } 0.8 \leq X \leq 0.9) = 0.1 + 0.1 = 0.2$. (e) $P(\text{not } [0.3 \leq X \leq 0.8]) = 1 - 0.5 = 0.5$. (f) $P(X = 0.5) = 0$.

7.6 (a) The 36 possible pairs of "up faces" are:

$$(1, 1) \quad (1, 2) \quad (1, 3) \quad (1, 4) \quad (1, 5) \quad (1, 6)$$
$$(2, 1) \quad (2, 2) \quad (2, 3) \quad (2, 4) \quad (2, 5) \quad (2, 6)$$
$$(3, 1) \quad (3, 2) \quad (3, 3) \quad (3, 4) \quad (3, 5) \quad (3, 6)$$
$$(4, 1) \quad (4, 2) \quad (4, 3) \quad (4, 4) \quad (4, 5) \quad (4, 6)$$
$$(5, 1) \quad (5, 2) \quad (5, 3) \quad (5, 4) \quad (5, 5) \quad (5, 6)$$
$$(6, 1) \quad (6, 2) \quad (6, 3) \quad (6, 4) \quad (6, 5) \quad (6, 6)$$

(b) Each pair must have probability 1/36. (c) Let x = sum of up faces. Then

Sum Outcomes	Probability
$x = 2$ (1, 1)	$p = 1/36$
$x = 3$ (1, 2) (2, 1)	$p = 2/36$
$x = 4$ (1, 3) (2, 2) (3, 1)	$p = 3/36$
$x = 5$ (1, 4) (2, 3) (3, 2) (4, 1)	$p = 4/36$
$x = 6$ (1, 5) (2, 4) (3, 3) (4, 2) (5, 1)	$p = 5/36$
$x = 7$ (1, 6) (2, 5) (3, 4) (4, 3) (5, 2) (6, 1)	$p = 6/36$
$x = 8$ (2, 6) (3, 5) (4, 4) (5, 3) (6, 2)	$p = 5/36$
$x = 9$ (3, 6) (4, 5) (5, 4) (6, 3)	$p = 4/36$
$x = 10$ (4, 6) (5, 5) (6, 4)	$p = 3/36$
$x = 11$ (5, 6) (6, 5)	$p = 2/36$
$x = 12$ (6, 6)	$p = 1/36$

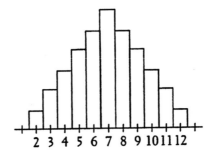

(d) p (7 or 11) = 6/36 + 2/36 = 8/36 or 2/9 (e) p (any sum other than 7) = $1 - p$ (7) = $1 - 6/36 = 30/36 = 5/6$ by the complement rule.

7.7 (a) All probabilities are between 0 and 1; the probabilities add to 1. Histogram below.

(b) $P(X \geq 5) = 0.07 + 0.03 + 0.01 = 0.11$.

(c) $P(X > 5) = 0.03 + 0.01 = 0.04$.

(d) $P(2 < X \leq 4) = 0.17 + 0.15 = 0.32$.

(e) $P(X \neq 1) = 1 - 0.25 = 0.75$.

(f) Write either $X \geq 3$ or $X > 2$. The probability is $1 - (0.25 + 0.32) = 0.43$.

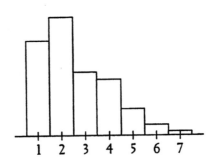

7.8 (a) 75.2%. (b) All probabilities are between 0 and 1; the probabilities add to 1. (c) $P(X \geq 6) = 1 - 0.010 - 0.007 = 0.983$. (d) $P(X > 6) = 1 - 0.010 - 0.007 - 0.007 = 0.976$. (e) Either $X \geq 9$ or $X > 8$. The probability is $0.068 + 0.070 + 0.041 + 0.752 = 0.931$.

7.9 (a) $(0.6)(0.6)(0.4) = 0.144$. (b) The possible combinations are SSS, SSO, SOS, OSS, SOO, OSO, OOS, OOO (S = support, O = oppose). $P(SSS) = 0.6^3 = 0.216$, $P(SSO) = P(SOS) = P(OSS) = (0.6^2)(0.4) = 0.144$, $P(SOO) = P(OSO) = P(OOS) = (0.6)(0.4^2) = 0.096$, and $P(OOO) = 0.4^3 = 0.064$. (c) The distribution is given in the table. The probabilities are found by adding the probabilities from (b), noting that (e.g.) $P(X = 1) = P(SSO$ or SOS or $OSS)$. (d) Write either $X \geq 2$ or $X > 1$. The probability is $0.288 + 0.064 = 0.352$.

Value of X	0	1	2	3
Probability	0.216	0.432	0.288	0.064

7.10 (a) The height should be $\frac{1}{2}$, since the area under the curve must be 1. The density curve is below. (b) $P(y \leq 1) = \frac{1}{2}$, (c) $P(0.5 < y < 1.3) = 0.4$. (d) $P(y \geq 0.8) = 0.6$.

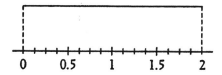

7.11 (a) The area of a triangle is $\frac{1}{2}bh = \frac{1}{2}(2)(1) = 1$. (b) $P(Y < 1) = 0.5$. (c) $P(Y < 0.5) = 0.125$.

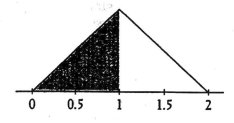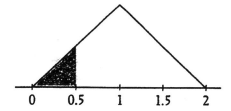

7.12 (TI-83) The resulting histogram should *approximately* resemble the triangular density curve of Figure 7.8, with any deviations or irregularities depending upon the specific random numbers generated.

7.13 (a) $P(\hat{p} \geq 0.5) = P(Z \geq \frac{0.5 - 0.3}{0.023}) = P(Z \geq 8.7) = 0$. (b) $P(\hat{p} < 0.25) = P(Z < -2.17) = 0.0150$. (c) $P(0.25 \leq \hat{p} \leq 0.35) = P(-2.17 \leq Z \leq 2.17) = 0.9700$.

7.14 (TI-83) For a *sample* simulation of 400 observations from the N(0.3, 0.023) observations: there are 4 observations less than 0.25, so the relative frequency is $4/400 = .01$. The actual probability that $p < .25$ is .0149.

7.15 (a) $P(\hat{p} \geq 0.16) = P(Z \geq \frac{0.16 - 0.15}{0.0092}) = P(Z \geq 1.09) = 0.1379$. (b) $P(0.14 \leq \hat{p} \leq 0.16) = P(-1.09 \leq Z \leq 1.09) = 0.7242$.

7.16 (TI-83) In this case, we will simulate 500 observations from the N(.15, .0092) distribution. The required TI-83 commands are as follows:

```
ClrList L₁
randNorm (.15, .0092, 500) → L₁
sortA(L₁)
```

Scrolling through the 500 simulated observations, we can determine the relative frequency of observations that are at least .16 by using the complement rule. For a sample simulation, there are 435 observations less than .16, thus the desired relative frequency is $1 - 435/500 = 65/500 = .13$. The actual probability that $p \geq .16$ is .1385. 500 observations yield a reasonably close approximation.

SECTION 7.2

7.17 $\mu = (0)(0.10) + (1)(0.15) + (2)(0.30) + (3)(0.30) + (4)(0.15) = 2.25$.

7.18 (a) The payoff is either $0 or $3; see table below. (b) For each $1 bet, $\mu_x = (\$0)(0.75) + (\$3)(0.25) = \$0.75$. (c) The casino makes 25 cents for every dollar bet (in the long run).

Value of X	0	3
Probability	0.75	0.25

7.19 If your number is *abc*, then of the 1000 three-digit numbers, there are six — *abc, acb, bac, bca, cab, cba* — for which you will win the box. Therefore, we win nothing with probability $\frac{994}{1000} = 0.994$ and win $83.33 with probability $\frac{6}{1000} = 0.006$. The expected payoff on a $1 bet is $\mu = (\$0)(0.994) + (\$83.33)(0.006) = \$0.50$.

7.20 (TI-83) The graph for $x_{max} = 10$ displays visible variation for the first ten values of x, whereas the graph for $x_{max} = 100$ gets closer and closer to $\mu = 64.5$ as x increases. This illustrates that the larger the sample size (represented by the integers 1, 2, 3, ... in L_1), the closer the sample means x get to the population mean $\mu = 64.5$. (In other words, this exercise illustrates the law of large numbers in a graphical manner.)

7.21 Below is the probability distribution for L, the length of the longest run of heads or tails. $P(\text{You win}) = P(\text{run of 1 or 2}) = \frac{89}{512} = 0.1738$, so the expected outcome is $\mu = (\$2)(0.1738) + (-\$1)(0.8262) = -\$0.4785$. On the average, you will lose about 48 cents each time you play. (Simulated results should be close to this exact result; how close depends on how many trials are used.)

Value of L	1	2	3	4	5	6	7	8	9	10
Probability	$\frac{1}{512}$	$\frac{88}{512}$	$\frac{185}{512}$	$\frac{127}{512}$	$\frac{63}{512}$	$\frac{28}{512}$	$\frac{12}{512}$	$\frac{5}{512}$	$\frac{2}{512}$	$\frac{1}{512}$

7.22 (a) The wheel is not affected by its past outcomes — it has no memory; outcomes are independent. So on any one spin, black and red remain equally likely. (b) Removing a card changes the composition of the remaining deck, so successive draws are not independent. If you hold 5 red cards, the deck now contains 5 fewer red cards, so your chance of another red decreases.

7.23 No: Assuming all "at-bat"s are independent of each other, the 35% figure only applies to the "long run" of the season, not to "short runs."

7.24 The total mean is $40 + 5 + 25 = 70$ minutes.

7.25 (a) Independent: Weather conditions a year apart should be independent. (b) Not independent: Weather patterns tend to persist for several days; today's weather tells us something about tomorrow's. (c) Not independent: The two locations are very close together, and would likely have similar weather conditions.

7.26 (a) The total mean is $11 + 20 = 31$ seconds. (b) No: Changing the standard deviations does not affect the means. (c) No: The total mean does not depend on dependence or independence of the two variables.

7.27 In 4.51, we had $\mu = 2.25$, so $\sigma_x^2 = (0 - 2.25)^2(0.10) + (1 - 2.25)^2(0.15) + (2 - 2.25)^2(0.30) + (3 - 2.25)^2(0.30) + (4 - 2.25)^2(0.15) = 1.3875$, and $\sigma_x = \sqrt{1.3875} = 1.178$.

7.28 (a) $\mu_x = (0)(0.03) + (1)(0.16) + (2)(0.30) + (3)(0.23) + (4)(0.17) + (5)(0.11) = 2.68$. $\sigma_x^2 = (0 - 2.68)^2(0.03) + (1 - 2.68)^2(0.16) + (2 - 2.68)^2(0.30) + (3 - 2.68)^2(0.23) + (4 - 2.68)^2 (0.17) + (5 - 2.68)^2(0.11) = 1.7176$, and $\sigma_x = \sqrt{1.7176} = 1.3106$.

(b) To simulate (say) 500 observations of x, we will first simulate 500 random integers between 1 and 100 by using the TI-83 commands:

$$\text{randInt}(1,100,500) \rightarrow L_1$$

The command sortA(L_1) sorts these random observations in increasing order. We now identify 500 observations of x as follows:

Integers	1 to 3	correspond to	$x = 0$
	4 to 19		$x = 1$
	20 to 49		$x = 2$
	50 to 72		$x = 3$
	73 to 89		$x = 4$
	90 to 100		$x = 5$

For a sample run of the simulation, we obtain

12	observations of	$x = 0$
86		$x = 1$
155		$x = 2$
118		$x = 3$
75		$x = 4$
54		$x = 5$

These data yield a sample mean and standard deviation of $\bar{x} = 2.64$, $s = 1.292$, very close to μ, σ.

7.29 Since the two times are independent, the total variance is $\sigma_{total}^2 = \sigma_{pos}^2 + \sigma_{att}^2 = 2^2 + 4^2 = 20$, so $\sigma_{total} = \sqrt{20} = 4.472$ seconds.

7.30 Since the two times are independent, the total variance is $\sigma_{total}^2 = \sigma_{first}^2 + \sigma_{second}^2 = 2^2 + 1^2 = 5$, so $\sigma_{total} = \sqrt{5} = 2.236$ minutes.

7.31 (a) Randomly selected students would presumably be unrelated. (b) $\mu_{f-m} = \mu_f - \mu_m = 120 - 105 = 15$. $\sigma_{f-m}^2 = \sigma_f^2 + \sigma_m^2 = 28^2 + 35^2 = 2009$, so $\sigma_{f-m} = 44.82$. (c) Knowing only the mean and standard deviation, we cannot find that probability (unless we assume that the distribution is normal). Many different distribution can have the same mean and standard deviation.

7.32 (a) $\mu_x = 550°$ Celsius; $\sigma_x^2 = 32.5$, so $\sigma_x = 5.701°$ C. (b) Mean: $0°$ C; standard deviation: $5.701°$ C. (c) $\mu_y = \frac{9}{5}\mu_x + 32 = 1022°$ F, and $\sigma_y = \frac{9}{5}\sigma_x = 10.26°$ F.

7.33 Read two-digit random numbers. Establish the correspondence 01 to 10 ↔ 540°, 11 to 35 ↔ 545°, 36 to 65 ↔ 550°, 66 to 90 ↔ 555°, and 91 to 99, 00 ↔ 560°. Repeat many times, and record the corresponding temperatures. Average the temperatures to approximate μ; find the standard deviations of the temperatures to approximate σ.

CHAPTER REVIEW

7.34 The missing probability is 0.99058 (so that the sum is 1). This gives mean earnings $\mu_x =$ \$303.3525.

7.35 The mean μ of the company's "winnings" (premiums) and their "losses" (insurance claims) is positive. Even though the company will lose a large amount of money on a small number of policyholders who die, it will gain a small amount on the majority. The law of large numbers says that the average "winnings" minus "losses" should be close to μ, and overall the company will almost certainly show a profit.

7.36 (a) Not independent: Knowing the total X of the first two cards tells us something about the total Y for three cards. (b) Independent: Separate rolls of the dice should be independent.

7.37 (a) A single random digit simulates each toss, with (say) odd = heads and even = tails. The first round is two digits, with two odds a win; if you don't win, look at two more digits, again with two odds a win. (b) The probability of winning is $\frac{1}{4} + \left(\frac{3}{4}\right)\left(\frac{1}{4}\right) = \frac{7}{16}$, so the expected value is $(\$1)\left(\frac{7}{16}\right) + (-\$1)\left(\frac{9}{16}\right) = -\frac{2}{16} = -\$0.125$.

7.38 (a) To do one repetition, start at any point in Table B and begin reading digits. As in Example 5.21, let the digits 0, 1, 2, 3, 4 = girl and 5, 6, 7, 8, 9 = boy, and read a string of digits until a "0 to 4" (girl) appears or until four consecutive "5 to 9"s (boys) have appeared, whichever comes first. Then let the observation of x = number of children for this repetition = the number of digits in the string you have read. Repeat this procedure 25 times to obtain your 25 observations.

(b) The possible outcomes and their corresponding values of x = number of children are as follows:

	Outcome	
$x = 1$	G	(first child is a girl)
$x = 2$	BG	(second child is a girl)
$x = 3$	BBG	(third child is a girl)
$x = 4$	BBBG, BBBB	(four children)

Using the facts that births are independent, the fact that B and G are equally likely to occur on any one birth, and the multiplication rule for independent events, we find that

$$
\begin{aligned}
p(x = 1) &= 1/2 \\
p(x = 2) &= (1/2)(1/2) = 1/4 \\
p(x = 3) &= (1/2)(1/2)(1/2) = 1/8 \\
p(x = 4) &= (1/2)(1/2)(1/2)(1/2) + (1/2)(1/2)(1/2)(1/2) \\
&= 1/16 + 1/16 = 1/8
\end{aligned}
$$

The probability distribution of x is therefore:

x_i	1	2	3	4
p_i	1/2	1/4	1/8	1/8

(c) $\mu_x = \Sigma x_i p_i$
$= (1)(1/2) + (2)(1/4) + (3)(1/8) + (4)(1/8)$
$= 1/2 + 1/2 + 3/8 + 1/2$
$= 1.875$

7.39 The two histograms are superimposed below. Means: $\mu_H = 2.6$ and $\mu_F = 3.14$ persons. Variances: $\sigma_H^2 = 2.02$ and $\sigma_F^2 = 1.5604$. Standard deviations: $\sigma_H = 1.421$ and $\sigma_F = 1.249$ persons.

Since families must include at least two people, it is not too surprising that the average family is slightly larger (about 0.54 persons) than the average household. For large family/household sizes, the differences between the distributions are small.

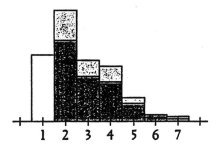

7.40 $\mu_X = (\mu - \sigma)(0.5) + (\mu + \sigma)(0.5) = \mu$, and $\sigma_X = \sigma$ since $\sigma_X^2 = [\mu - (\mu - \sigma)]^2(0.5) = [\mu - (\mu + \sigma)]^2(0.5) = \sigma^2(0.5) + \sigma^2(0.5) = \sigma^2$.

7.41 (a) $\sigma_Y^2 = (300 - 445)^2(0.4) + (500 - 445)^2(0.5) + (750 - 455)^2(0.1) = 19.225$ and $\sigma_Y = 138.65$ units. (b) $\sigma_{X+Y}^2 = \sigma_X^2 + \sigma_Y^2 = 7,800,000 + 19,225 = 7,819,225$, so $\sigma_{X+Y} = 2796.29$ units. (c) $\sigma_Z^2 = \sigma_{2000X}^2 + \sigma_{3500Y}^2 = (2000)^2\sigma_X^2 + (3500)^2\sigma_Y^2$, so $\sigma_Z = \$5,606,738$.

7.42 (a) $\mu_{Y-X} = \mu_Y - \mu_X = 2.001 - 2.000 = 0.001$ g. $\sigma_{Y-X}^2 = \sigma_Y^2 + \sigma_X^2 = 0.002^2 + 0.001^2 = 0.000005$, so $\sigma_{Y-X} = 0.002236$ g. (b) $\mu_Z = \frac{1}{2}\mu_X + \frac{1}{2}\mu_Y = 2.0005$ g. $\sigma_Z^2 = \frac{1}{4}\sigma_X^2 + \frac{1}{4}\sigma_Y^2 = 0.00000125$, so $\sigma_Z = 0.001118$ g. Z is slightly more variable than Y, since $\sigma_Y < \sigma_Z$.

7.43 $\sigma_X^2 = 94,236,826.64$, so that $\sigma_X = \$9707.57$.

7.44 (a) $\mu_T = \mu_X + \mu_Y = 2\mu_X = \$606.705$. $\sigma_T = \sqrt{\sigma_X^2 + \sigma_Y^2} = \sqrt{2\sigma_X^2} = \$13,728.57$. (b) $\mu_Z = \frac{1}{2}\mu_T = \mu_X = \$303.3525$. $\sigma_Z = \sqrt{\frac{1}{4}\sigma_X^2 + \frac{1}{4}\sigma_Y^2} = \sqrt{\frac{1}{2}\sigma_X^2} = \$6864.29$. (c) With this new definition of Z: $\mu_Z = \mu_X = \$303.3525$ (unchanged). $\sigma_Z = \sqrt{\frac{1}{4}\sigma_X^2} = \frac{1}{2}\sigma_X = \$4853.78$ (smaller by a factor of $1/\sqrt{2}$).

The Binomial and Geometric Distributions

SECTION 8.1

8.1 It may be binomial if we assume that there are no twins or other multiple births among the next 20 (this would violate requirement 2 — independence — of the binomial setting), and that for all births, the probability that the baby is female is the same (requirement 4).

8.2 No — the number of observations is not fixed.

8.3 No — since she receives instruction after incorrect answers, her probability of success is likely to increase.

8.4 Assuming that Joe's chance of winning the lottery is the same every week, and that a year consists of 52 weeks (observations), this would be binomial.

8.5 (a) .2637 (b) The binomial probabilities for $x = 0, \ldots, 5$ are: .2373, .3955, .2637, .0879, .0146, .0010. (e) The cumulative probabilities for $x = 0, \ldots, 5$ are: .2373, .6328, .8965, .9844, .9990, 1. Compared with Corinne's cdf histogram, the bars in this histogram get taller, sooner. Both peak at 1 on the extreme right.

8.6 (TI-83) We enter the values of x = number of gaskets made into list L_1 by using the command seq (X, X, 0, 12) $\rightarrow L_1$. Then we enter the binomial probabilities into list L_2 by using binompdf (12, .75, L_1) $\rightarrow L_2$. The command cumSum (L_2) $\rightarrow L_3$ computes the cumulative distribution of X and stores it in list L_3. The command bionomcdf (12, .75, L_1) $\rightarrow L_4$ yields the exact same results.

8.7 (a) The distribution of $X = B(7, .5)$ is symmetric; the shape depends on the value of the probability of success. Since .5 is halfway between 0 and 1, the histogram is symmetric.

(b) With the values of $X = 0, 1, \ldots, 7$ in L_1, define L_2 to be bionomcdf(7, .5). Then the probability table for $B(7, .5)$ is installed in L_1 and L_2. Here is a histogram of the p.d.f.:

 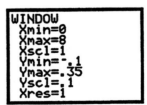 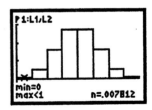

(c) $P(X = 7) = .0078125$, as shown.

8.8 (a) $\binom{15}{3}(0.3)^3(0.7)^{12} = 0.17004$. (b) $\binom{15}{0}(0.3)^0(0.7)^{15} + \cdots + \binom{15}{3}(0.3)^3(0.7)^{12} = 0.29687$.

8.9 $P(X = 10) = \binom{20}{10}(0.8)^{10}(0.2)^{10} = 0.00203$.

8.10 (a) $n = 10$ and $p = 0.25$. (b) $\binom{10}{2}(0.25)^2(0.75)^8 = 0.28157$. (c) $P(X \leq 2) = \binom{10}{0}(0.25)^0(0.75)^{10} + \cdots + \binom{10}{2}(0.25)^2(0.75)^8 = 0.52559$.

8.11 There are $n = 15$ people on the committee, and the probability that a randomly selected person is Hispanic is $p = .3$. Let 0, 1, 2 $\leftrightarrow$ Hispanic and let 3–9 $\leftrightarrow$ non-Hispanic. Use the random digit table. Or, using the TI-83, repeat the command 30 times: randBin(1, .3, 15) $\rightarrow$ L$_1$: sum(L$_1$) $\rightarrow$ L$_2$ (1) where 0 = non-Hispanic, and 1 = Hispanic. Our frequencies were:

	1	2	4	5	11	3	4	
0	1	2	3	4	5	6	7	8

The relative frequency of 3 or fewer Hispanics is 7/30 = .233. Compare this with the theoretical result: $P(X \leq 3) = 0.29687$, where X = number of Hispanics on the committee.

8.12 In this case, $n = 20$ and the probability that a randomly selected basketball player graduates is $p = .8$. We will estimate $p(X \geq 10)$ by simulating 30 observations of X = number graduated and computing the relative frequency of observations that are 10 or greater. The sequence of TI-83 commands is as follows: randBin (1, .8, 20) $\rightarrow$ L$_1$: sum(L$_1$) $\rightarrow$ L$_2$ (1), where 1's represent players who graduated. (Press ENTER sufficient times to obtain 30 numbers.) For a sample simulation, the following observations are obtained:

16	16	15	16	14	18
14	16	17	12	16	15
15	16	18	12	15	17
19	18	17	14	16	15
17	14	16	18	17	16

Thus, $p(X \geq 10) = 30/30 = 1.000$. The actual value of $P(X \geq 10)$ is 1-binomcdf(20, .8, 9) = .9994 ≈ 1.

8.13 The sample size is $n = 10$, and the probability that a randomly selected employed woman has never been married is $p = 0.25$. Let 0 $\leftrightarrow$ never married, let 1, 2, 3, $\leftrightarrow$ married, and use Table B. Or, using the TI-83, repeat the command randBin(1, .25, 10) $\rightarrow$ L$_1$: sum(L$_1$). Our results for 30 repetitions were:

2	3	14	5	4	2
0	1	2	3	4	5

The relative frequency of 2 or fewer never married is 19/30 = .63. The actual value of $P(X \le 2) =$ `binomcdf(10, .25, 2)` = .525.

8.14 $\mu = \frac{5}{4} = 1.25$, $\sigma = \sqrt{\frac{15}{16}} = 0.96825$.

8.15 (a) $\mu = 4.5$. (b) $\sigma = \sqrt{3.15} = 1.77482$. (c) If $p = 0.1$, then $\sigma = \sqrt{1.35} = 1.16190$. If $p = 0.01$, then $\sigma = \sqrt{0.1485} = 0.38536$. As p gets close to 0, σ gets closer to 0.

8.16 (a) $\mu = 16$ (if $p = 0.8$). (b) $\sigma = \sqrt{3.2} = 1.78885$. (c) If $p = 0.9$, then $\sigma = \sqrt{1.8} = 1.34164$. If $p = 0.99$, then $\sigma = \sqrt{0.198} = 0.44497$. As p gets close to 1, σ gets closer to 0.

8.17 $\mu = 2.5$, $\sigma = \sqrt{1.875} = 1.36931$.

8.18 (a) We simulate 10 observations of X = number of defective switches (for which $n = 10$, $p = .1$) by using the command `randBin(1, .1, 10)` $\rightarrow$ L$_1$: sum (L$_1$) $\rightarrow$ L$_2$ (1). (Press ENTER 10 times.) The observations for one sample simulation are: 0, 0, 4, 0, 1, 0, 1, 0, 0, 1. For these data, $\bar{x} = .7$. To generate 25/50 observations of x, replace 10 with 25/50 in the `randBin` command above. As the number of observations increases, the resulting $\bar{x}$ should approximate the known mean $\mu = 1$ more closely, by the law of large numbers. (b) Simulate 10 observations of X = number of free throws Corinne makes (where the number of trials is $n = 12$ and the probability of a basket on a given trial is $p = .75$) by using the command `randBin(1, .75, 12)` $\rightarrow$ L$_1$: sum(L$_1$) $\rightarrow$ L$_2$(1). (Press ENTER 10 times.) The observations for one sample simulation are: 9, 8, 10, 10, 9, 8, 10, 9, 8, 8. For these data, $\bar{x} = 8.9$. Compare this with the known mean $\mu = np = (12)(.75) = 9$. To generate 25/50 observations of $\bar{x}$, replace 10 with 25/50 in the `randBin` command above. As the number of observations increases, the resulting $\bar{x}$ should approximate the known mean $\mu = 1$ more closely, by the law of large numbers.

8.19 (a) $n = 20$ and $p = 0.25$. (b) $\mu = 5$. (c) $\binom{20}{5}(0.25)^5(0.75)^{15} = 0.20233$.

8.20 (a) $n = 6$ and $p = 0.65$. (b) X takes values from 0 to 6. (c) $P(X = 0) = 0.00184$, $P(X = 1) 0.02048$, $P(X = 2) = 0.09510$, $P(X = 3) = 0.23549$, $P(X = 4) = 0.32801$, $P(X = 5) = 0.24366$, $P(X = 6) = 0.07542$, (d) $\mu = 3.9$, $\sigma = \sqrt{1.365} = 1.16833$.

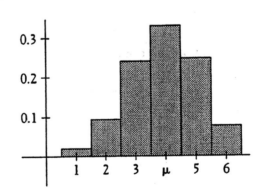

8.21 (a) The probability that all are assessed as truthful is $\binom{12}{0}(0.2)^0(0.8)^{12} = 0.06872$; the probability that at least one is reported to be a liar is $1 - 0.06872 = 0.93128$. (b) $\mu = 2.4$, $\sigma = \sqrt{1.92} = 1.38564$.

8.22 (a) X has a binomial distribution with $n = 20$ and $p = 0.99$. (b) $P(X = 20) = 0.81791$; $P(X < 20) = 0.18209$. (c) $\mu = 19.8$, $\sigma = \sqrt{0.198} = 0.44497$.

8.23 (a) $P(\text{switch is bad}) = \frac{1000}{10000} = 0.1$; $P(\text{switch is OK}) = \frac{9000}{10000} = 0.9$. (b) 9999 switches remain, of which 999 are bad. Under these conditions, $P(\text{switch is bad}) = \frac{999}{9999} = 0.09990999. . .$, and $P(\text{switch is OK}) = \frac{9000}{9999} = 0.90009000. . . .$ (c) Again, 9999 switches remain; this time 1000 are bad, so that $P(\text{switch is bad}) = \frac{1000}{9999} = 0.10001000. . .$, and $P(\text{switch is OK}) = \frac{8999}{9999} = 0.89998999. . . .$

SECTION 8.2

8.24 (a) Geometric setting; success = tail, failure = head; trial = flip of coin; $p = 1/2$. (b) Not a geometric setting. You are not counting the number of trials before the first success is obtained. (c) Geometric setting; success = jack, failure = any other card; trial = drawing of a card; $p = 4/52 = 1/13$. (Trials are independent because the card is replaced each time.) (d) Geometric setting, success = match all 6 numbers, failure = do not match all 6 numbers; trial = drawing on a particular day; the probability of success is the same for each trial; and trials are independent because the setting of a drawing is always the same and the results on different drawings do not influence each other. (e) Not a geometric setting. The trials (draws) are not independent because you are drawing without replacement. Also, you are interested in getting 3 successes, rather than just the first success.

8.25 (a) The four conditions of a geometric setting hold, with probability of success = 1/2. ·

(b) and (d)

X	1	2	3	4	5	. . .
P(X)	.5	.25	.125	.0625	.03125	
c.d.f.	.5	.75	.875	.9375	.96875	

(c)

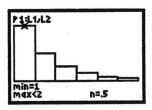

(e) Sum $= \dfrac{a}{1-r} = \dfrac{.5}{1-r} = 1$

8.26 (a) X = number of drives tested in order to find the first defective. Success = defective drive. This is a geometric setting because the trials (tests) on successive drives are independent, $p = .03$ on each trial, and X is counting the number of trials required to achieve the first success.

(b) $P(X = 5) = (1 - .03)^{5-1}(.03)$
$= (.97)^4(.03)$
$= .0266$

(c)

X	1	2	3	4
P(X)	.03	.0291	.0282	.0274

8.27

X	p.d.f.	c.d.f.
1	.5	.5
2	.25	.75
3	.125	.825
4	.0625	.9375
5	.03125	.96875

Histograms for the p.d.f. and c.d.f. are:

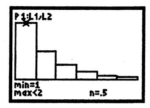 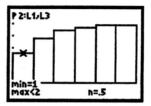

8.28 (a) The cumulative distribution histogram (out to $X = 10$) for rolling a die is shown below. Note that the cumulative function value for $X = 10$ is only .8385. Many more bars are needed for it to reach a height of 1.

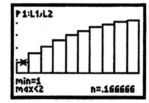 

(b) $P(X > 6) = (1 - 1/6)^6 = (5/6)^6 = .3349$. (c) The smallest positive integer k for which $P(X \leq k) > .99$ is $k = 26$ (see second calculator screen above).

8.29 (a) Assumptions needed for the geometric model to apply are that the shots are independent, and that the probability of success is the same for each shot. A "success" is a missed shot, so the probability of success is $p = 0.2$. The four conditions for a geometric setting are satisfied. (b) The first "success" (miss) is the sixth shot, so $X = 6$ and $P(X = 6) = (1 - p)^{n-1} p = (.8)^5(.2) = .0655$. (c) $P(X \leq 5) = 1 - (1-p)^n = 1 - (0.8)^6 = 0.738$

8.30 (a) Geometric setting; $X =$ number of marbles you must draw to find the first red marble. We choose geometric in this case because the number of trials (draws) is the variable quantity.

(b) $P = 20/35 \quad = 4/7$ in this case, so
$P(X = 2) \quad = (1 - 4/7)^{2-1}(4/7) = (3/7)(4/7) = 12/49 = .2449$
$P(X \leq 2) \quad = 4/7 + (3/7)(4/7) = 4/7 + 12/49 = 40/49 = .8163$
$P(X > 2) \quad = (1 - 4/7)^2 = (3/7)^2 = 9/49 = .1837$

(c) Use the commands seq(X, X, 1, 20) $\rightarrow$ L₁, geometpdf(4/7, L₁) $\rightarrow$ L₂, cumSum (L₂) $\rightarrow$ L₃ (or geometcdf(4/7, L₁) $\rightarrow$ L₃).

X	1	2	3	4	5	6	7	8	9	10
P(X)	.571	.245	.105	.045	.019	.008	.004	.002	.001	.000
F(X) c.d.f.	.571	.816	.921	.966	.986	.994	.997	.999	.99951	.9998

X	11	12	13	14	15	16	17	18	19	20
P(X)	.000	.000	.000	.000	.000	.000	.000	.000	.000	.000
F(X)	.9999	.9999	.9999	1	1	1	1	1	1	1

(d) The probability distribution histogram is Plot1; the cumulative distribution is Plot2.

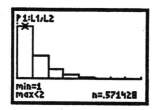 

8.31 No. The probability of success changes with each marble drawn.

8.32 (a) Success = getting a correct answer. X = number of questions Carla must answer in order to get the first correct answer. $p = 1/5 = .2$ (all 5 choices equally likely to be selected)

(b) $P(X = 5) = (1 - 1/5)^{5-1} (1/5) = (4/5)^4(1/5) = .082$.

(c) $P(X > 4) = (1 - 1/5)^4 = (4/5)^4 = .4096$.

(d)

X	1	2	3	4	5	....
P(X)	.2	.16	.128	.1024	.082	....

(e) $\mu_x = 1/(1/5) = 5$

8.33 (a) If "success" = son and p (success) = .5, then the average number of children per family is $\mu = 1/p = 1/.5 = 2$. (b) If the average size of the family is 2, and the last child is a boy, then the average number of girls per family is 1. (c) Let even digit = boy, and odd digit = girl. Read random digits until an even digit occurs. Count number of digits read. Repeat many times, and average the counts. Beginning on line 101 in the random digit table and simulating 50 trials, the average number of children per family is 1.96, and the average number of girls is .96. These are very close to the expected values.

8.34 (a) Letting G = girl and B = boy, the outcomes are: {G, BG, BBG, BBBG, BBBB}. Success = having a girl.

(b) X = number of boys can take values of 0, 1, 2, 3, or 4. The probabilities are calculated by using the multiplication rule for independent events:

$P(X = 0) = 1/2$
$P(X = 1) = (1/2)(1/2) = 1/4$
$P(X = 2) = (1/2)(1/2)(1/2) = 1/8$
$P(X = 3) = (1/2)(1/2)(1/2)(1/2) = 1/16$
$P(X = 4) = (1/2)(1/2)(1/2)(1/2) = 1/16$

X	0	1	2	3	4
P(X)	1/2	1/4	1/8	1/16	1/16

Note that $\Sigma P(X) = 1$.

(c) Let Y = number of children produced until first girl is seen. Then Y is a geometric variable for $Y = 1$ up to $Y = 4$, but then "stops" because the couple plans to stop at 4 children if it does not see a girl by that time. By the multiplication rule,

$P(Y = 1) = 1/2$
$P(Y = 2) = 1/4$
$P(Y = 3) = 1/8$
$P(Y = 4) = 1/16$

Note that the event {Y = 4} can only include the outcome BBBG. BBBB must be discarded. The probability distribution table would begin

Y	1	2	3	4
P(Y)	1/2	1/4	1/8	1/16

But note that this table is incomplete and this is not a valid probability model since $\Sigma \, P(Y) < 1$. The difficulty lies in the way Y was defined. It does not include the possible outcome BBBB.

(d) Let Z = number of children per family. Then

Z	1	2	3	4
P(Z)	1/2	1/4	1/8	1/16

and $\mu_Z = \Sigma \, Z \times P(Z) = (1)\,(1/2) + (2)\,(1/4) + (3)\,(1/8) + (4)\,(1/8)$
$= 1/2 + 1/2 + 3/8 + 1/2$
$= 1.875$

(e) $P(Z > 1.875) = P(2) + P(3) + P(4) = .5$ (f) The only way in which a girl cannot be obtained is BBBB, which has probability 1/16. Thus the probability of having a girl, by the complement rule, is $1 - 1/16 = 15/16 = .938$.

8.35 Let $0 - 4 \leftrightarrow$ girl and $5 - 9 \leftrightarrow$ boy. Beginning with line 130 in the random digit table:

```
690 | 51 | 64 | 81 | 7871 | 74 | 0 | 951 | 784
BBG   BG   BG   BG   BBBG   BG   G   BBG   BBG
 3     2    2    2     4     2   1    3     3
```

```
53 | 4 | 0 | 64 | 89872 | 0 | 1 | 972 | 4 | 50 | 50
BG   G   G   BG   BBBBG   G   G   BBG   G   BG   BG
 2   1   1   2      5     1   1    3    1   2    2
```

```
0 | 71 | 663 | 2 | 81
B   BG   BBG   G   BG
1   2     3    1   2
```

The average number of children is 52/25 = 2.08. This compares with the expected value of 1.875.

8.36 We will approximate the expected number of children, μ, by making the mean $\bar{x}$ of 25 randomly generated observations of X. We create a suitable string of random digits (say of length 100) by using the command randInt (0, 9, 100) $\rightarrow$ L_1. Now we scroll down the list L_1. Let the digits 0 to 4 represent a boy and 5 to 9 represent a girl. We read digits in the string until we get a "5 to 9" (girl) or until four "0 to 4"s (boys) are read, whichever comes first. In each case, we record X = the number of digits in the string = the number of children. We continue until 25 X-values have been recorded. A sample string L_1 yields the following values of X:

```
245 / 8 / 06 / 37 / 9 / 6 / 6 / 6 / 2443 / 9 / 9 / 16 / 45 /
(3)   (1)   (2)   (2)  (1) (1) (1) (1)  (4)   (1) (1) (2)  (2)
```

```
8 / 336 / 15 / 9 / 1331 / 38 / 8 / 48 / 37 / 119 / 5 / 8 /
(1)  (3)   (2)  (1)  (4)   (2)  (1)  (2)  (2)   (3)  (1) (1)
```

This yields $\bar{x} = 45/25 = 1.8$, compared with the known mean $\mu = 1.875$.

CHAPTER REVIEW

8.37 P(alcohol related fatality) = 346/869 = .398. If X = number of alcohol related fatalities, then X is B(25, .398). $\mu = np = 25(.398) = 9.95$. $\sigma = \sqrt{((9.95)(.602))} = 2.45$. $P(X \le 5) = $ `binomcdf(25, .398, 5)` = .0307.

8.38 (a) There are 150 independent observations, each with probability of "success" (response) $p = .5$. (b) $\mu = np = (150)(0.5) = 75$. (c) `binomcdf(150, .5, 70)` = 0.2313. (d) $\mu = np$. 100 = $(n)(0.5)$, so $n = 200$.

8.39 (a) The four requirements of a binomial setting are satisfied. (b) $\mu = np = (200)(.4) = 80$ (c) Using the TI-83, $P(75 \le X \le 85) = $ `binomcdf(200, .4, 85)` $-$ `binomcdf(200, .4 .74)` = .5727 (d) $P(X \ge 100) = 1 - P(X \le 99) = 1 - $ `binomcdf(200, .4, 99)` = .0026.

8.40 (a) From the probability distribution table: $P(X = 6) = .3087$. (b) From the cumulative distribution table: $P(X \le 7) = .8764$. (c) $P(X < 7) = P(X \le 6) = .5811$. (d) $P(5 \le X \le 7) = P(X \le 7) - P(X \le 4) = .8764 - .0880 = .7884$. (e) $P((X < 3) \text{ or } (X > 6)) = P(X < 3) + P(X > 6) = P(X \le 2) + P(X \ge 7) = P(X \le 2) + P(X = 7) + P(X = 8) = .0027 + .2953 + .1236 = .4216$.

8.41 (a) Out of 8 possible outcomes, HHH and TTT do not produce winners. So P(no winner) = 2/8 = .25.

(b) P(winner) = 1 − .25 = .75.

(c) Let X = number of coin tosses until someone wins. Then X is geometric because all four conditions for a geometric setting are satisfied.

(d)

X	1	2	3	4	5	. . .
P(X)	.75	.1875	.04688	.01172	.00293	
c.d.f.	.75	.9375	.9844	.9961	.9990	

(e) $P(X \le 2) = .9375$ from the table. (f) $P(X \le 4) = .9961$. (g) $\mu = 1/p = 1/.75 = 1.33$. (h) Let 1 ↔ heads and 0 ↔ tails, and enter the command `randInt(0, 1, 3)` and press ENTER 25 times. In our simulation, we recorded the following frequencies:

X	1	2	3
Freq.	21	3	1
Rel. Freq.	.84	.12	.04

These compare with the calculated probabilities of .75, .1875, and .04688, respectively. A larger number of trials should result in somewhat better agreement (Law of Large Numbers).

8.42 (a) Recall that if p = probability of success, then $\mu = 1/p$. Then the table is as follows:

X	.1	.2	.3	.4	.5	.6	.7	.8	.9
Y	10	5	3.33	2.5	2	1.67	1.43	1.25	1.1

(b)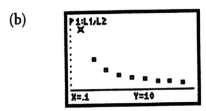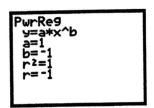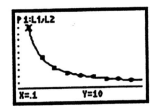

The equation of the power function is $\hat{y} = 1x^{-1} = 1/x$. The power function illustrates the fact that the mean of a geometric random variable is the *reciprocal* of the probability p of success: $\mu = 1/p$.

8.43 The larger the probability of success, the shorter the tail. If p is large (close to 1), then $(1 - p)$ will be small (close to 0), and consecutive integral powers of $(1 - p)$ will approach 0 rapidly. Then the product $(1 - p)^{n-1}p$ will also approach 0 rapidly. But this product is $P(X = n)$. So if p is large, you would expect a short tail in the histogram. Similar reasoning shows that if p is small, then you would expect a long tail.

8.44 X is geometric with $p = .325$. $1 - p = .675$. (a) $P(X = 1) = .325$ (b) $P(X \le 3) = .325 + (.675)(.325) + (.675)^2(.325) = .69245$ (c) $P(X > 4) = (.675)^4 = .208$ (d) The expected number of at-bats until Roberto gets his first hit is $\mu = 1/p = 1/.325 = 3.08$. (e) To do this, use the commands `seq(X, X, 1, 10)` $\rightarrow L_1$, `geometpdf(.325, L_1)` $\rightarrow L_2$, and `geometcdf(.325, L_1)` $\rightarrow L_3$. (f) The probability distribution histogram is Plot1; the cumulative distribution histogram is Plot 2.

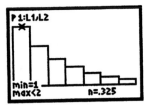 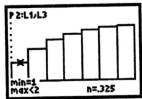

8.45 (a) In our simulation, we obtained the following results:

Outcome	1	2	3	4	5	6	7	8
Frequency	28	17	2	2				1
Rel. Freq.	.56	.34	.04	.04				.02

(b) We observed heads on the first toss 56% of the time. Our estimate of the probability of heads on the first toss is 0.5. (c) An estimate of the probability that the first head appears on an odd-numbered toss is 2/3.

9

Sampling Distributions

SECTION 9.1

9.1 7.2% is a statistic.

9.2 2.5003 is a parameter; 2.5009 is a statistic.

9.3 48% is a statistic; 52% is a parameter.

9.4 Both 335 and 289 are statistics.

9.5 The appearance of the histogram will vary from experiment to experiment. For comparison, here is the sampling distribution (assuming p really is 0.5). Answers for (b) will probably not resemble this much, but for (c), they may be fairly close.

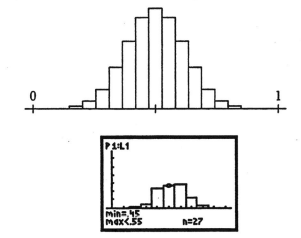

9.6 (a)

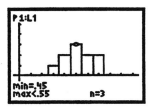

The results seem to be quite variable.

(b)

(c) The center is close to 0.5, and the shape is approximately normal.

(d) The spread of the distribution did not seem to change. To decrease the spread, I would increase the number of trials, n. For example, randBin(50, .5).

9.7 (a) The scores will vary depending on the starting row. Note that the smallest possible mean is 61.75 (from the sample 58, 62, 62, 65) and the largest is 77.25 (from 73, 74, 80, 82). Answers to (b) and (c) will vary; shown are two views of the sampling distribution. The first shows all possible values of the experiment (so the first rectangle is for 61.75, the next is for 62.00, etc.); the other shows values grouped from 61 to 61.75, 62 to 62.75, etc. (which makes the histogram less bumpy). The tallest rectangle in the first picture is 8 units; in the second, the tallest is 28 units.

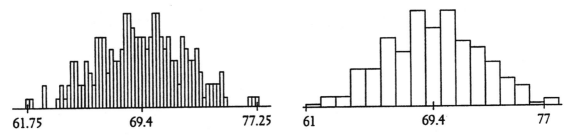

9.8 (a) Table is below; histogram not shown. (b) The histogram actually does *not* appear to have a normal shape. The sampling distribution is quite normal in appearance, but even a sample of size 100 does not *necessarily* show it. (c) The mean of $\hat{p}$ is 0.0981. The bias seems to be small. (d) The mean of the sampling distribution should be $p = 0.10$. (e) The mean would still be 0.10, but the spread would be smaller.

p	$\hat{p}$	Count	p	$\hat{p}$	Count	p	$\hat{p}$	Count
9	0.045	1	18	0.090	12	24	0.120	10
13	0.065	3	19	0.095	9	25	0.125	4
14	0.070	2	20	0.100	7	26	0.130	1
15	0.075	5	21	0.105	5	27	0.135	2
16	0.080	11	22	0.110	6	28	0.140	2
17	0.085	12	23	0.115	7	30	0.150	1

9.9 (a) Large bias and large variability. (b) Small bias and small variability. (c) Small bias, large variability. (d) Large bias, small variability.

9.10 (a) Since the smallest number of total tax returns (i.e., the smallest population) is still more than 100 times the sample size, the variability will be (approximately) the same for all states. (b) Yes, it will change — the sample taken from Wyoming will be about the same size, but the sample in, e.g., California will be considerably larger, and therefore the variability will decrease.

9.11 (a) The digits 00 to 100 represent shoppers. The digits 01 to 67 represent shoppers who find shopping frustrating. The program outputs the percent of shoppers who answer "Yes." (e) As the sample size increases, the variability decreases.

9.12 (a) Use digits 0 and 1 (or any other 2 of the 10 digits) to represent the presence of egg masses. Reading the first 10 digits from line 116, for example, gives YNNNN NNYNN — 2 square yards with egg masses, 8 without — so $\hat{p} = 0.2$. (b) The stemplot *might* look like the one below (which is close to the sampling distribution of $\hat{p}$). (c) The mean would be $p = 0.2$. (d) 0.4.

```
0.0 | 00
0.0 | 55555
0.1 | 000000
0.1 | 5555
0.2 | 00
0.2 | 5
```

9.13 (a) Use 0–3 to represent persons who would answer "yes." Looking at the first 20 digits on line 136 gives YNNYY NNNNY NNYNN YNNNN — 6 yes and 14 no, so $\hat{p} = 0.3$. (b) Most answers should fall between 0.3 and 0.5. (c) 0.4. (d) 0.5.

9.14 Assuming that the poll's sample size was less than 780,000 — 10% of the population of New Jersey — the variability would be practically the same for either population. (The sample size for this poll would have been considerably less than 780,000.)

SECTION 9.2

9.15 (a) $\mu = p = 0.15$, $\sigma = \sqrt{(0.15)(0.85) \div 1540} = 0.0091$. (b) The population (U.S. adults) is considerably larger than 10 times the sample size (1540). (c) $np = 231$, $n(1 - p) = 1309$ — both are much bigger than 10. (d) $P(0.13 < \hat{p} < 0.17) = P(-2.198 < Z < 2.198) = 0.9722$. (e) To achieve $\sigma = 0.0045$, we need a sample four times as large: 6160.

9.16 (a) $\mu = p = 0.4$, $\sigma = \sqrt{(0.4)(0.6) \div 1785} = 0.0116$. (b) The population (U.S. adults) is considerably larger than 10 times the sample size. (c) $np = 714$, $n(1 - p) = 1071$ — both are much bigger than 10. (d) $P(0.37 < \hat{p} < 0.43) = P(-2.586 < Z < 2.586) = 0.9904$. Over 99% of all samples should give $\hat{p}$ within ±3% of the true population proportion.

9.17 For $n = 200$: $\sigma = 0.02525$, and the probability is $P = 0.5704$. For $n = 800$: $\sigma = 0.01262$ and $P = 0.8858$. For $n = 3200$: $\sigma = 0.0631$ and $P = 0.9984$. Larger sample sizes give more accurate results (the sample proportions are more likely to be close to the true proportion).

9.18 For $n = 300$: $\sigma = 0.02828$ and $P = 0.7108$. For $n = 1200$: $\sigma = 0.01414$ and $P = 0.9660$. For $n = 4800$: $\sigma = 0.00707$ and $P = 1$ (approximately). Larger sample sizes give more accurate results (the sample proportions are more likely to be close to the true proportion).

9.19 (a) $\mu = 0.52$, $\sigma = 0.02234$. (b) np and $n(1 - p)$ are 260 and 240 respectively. $P(\hat{p} \geq 0.50) = P(Z \geq -0.8951) = 0.8159$.

9.20 (a) 0.86 (86%). (b) We use the normal approximation (Rule of Thumb 2 is *just* satisfied — $n(1 - p) = 10$). The standard deviation is 0.03, and $P(\hat{p} \leq 0.86) = P(Z \leq -1.33) = 0.0918$. (*Note:* The exact probability is 0.1239.) (c) Even when the claim is correct, there will be some variation in sample proportions. In particular, in about 10% of samples we can expect to observe 86 or fewer orders shipped on time.

9.21 Comparing the results of "Rule of Thumb 2," we see that it is clearly satisfied in the telephone number problem, and just barely satisfied in the mail-order problem — so the approximation is more accurate in the first of these.

9.22 (a) $np = 66$ and $n(1 - p) = 234$, so Rule of Thumb 2 is satisfied. $P(\hat{p} > 0.20) = P(Z > -0.8362) = 0.7985$. (b) $P(\hat{p} > 0.30) = P(Z > 3.345) = 0.0004$.

9.23 (a) $P(\hat{p} \leq 0.70) = P(Z \leq -1.155) = 0.1241$. (b) $P(\hat{p} \leq 0.70) = P(Z \leq -1.826) = 0.0339$. (c) The test must contain 400 questions. (d) The answer is the same for Laura.

9.24 (a) $np = 80$. (b) Still assuming that $p = 0.04$, $P(\hat{p} \geq \frac{75}{2000}) = P(Z \geq -0.57) = 0.7157$.

9.25 (a) $np = (15)(0.3) = 4.5$ — this fails Rule of Thumb 2. (b) The population size (316) is not at least 10 times as large as the sample size (50) — this fails Rule of Thumb 1.

SECTION 9.3

9.26 The mean for 4.17(b) is the population mean from 4.17(a), namely -3.5%. The standard deviation is $\sigma/\sqrt{n} = 26\%/\sqrt{5} = 11.628\%$.

9.27 Mean: 18.6, standard deviation: $5.9/\sqrt{76} = 0.67678$. The normality of individual scores is not necessary for this to be true.

9.28 Mean: 40.125, standard deviation: 0.001; normality is not needed.

9.29 Standard deviation: 0.04619.

9.30 (a) $P(X \geq 21) = P(Z \geq \frac{21-18.6}{5.9}) = P(Z \geq 0.4068) = 0.3421$. (b) $P(\bar{x} \geq 21) = P(Z \geq \frac{21-18.6}{5.9/\sqrt{50}}) = P(Z \geq 2.8764) = 0.0020$.

9.31 (a) $P(X < 295) = P(Z < -1) = 0.8413$. (b) $P(\bar{x} < 295) = P(Z < -2.4495) = 0.0072$.

9.32 (a) $N(123, 0.04619)$. (b) $P(Z > 21.65)$ — essentially 0.

9.33 $\bar{x}$ has approximately a $N(1.6, 0.0849)$ distribution; the probability is $P(Z > 4.71)$ — essentially 0.

9.34 $\bar{x}$ (the mean return) has approximately a $N(9\%, 4.174\%)$ distribution; $P(\bar{x} > 15\%) = P(Z > 1.437) = 0.9247$; $P(\bar{x} < 5\%) = P(Z < -0.9583) = 0.1690$.

9.35 The mean μ of the company's "winnings" (premiums) and their "losses" (insurance claims) is positive. Even though the company will lose a large amount of money on a small number of policyholders who die, it will gain a small amount on the majority. The law of large numbers guarantees that the average "winnings" minus "losses" will be close to μ, and overall the company will almost certainly show a profit.

9.36 (a) $N(55000, 4500/\sqrt{8}) = N(55000, 1591)$. (b) $P(Z < -2.011) = 0.0222$.

9.37 (a) $N(2.2, 0.1941)$. (b) $P(Z < -1.0304) = 0.1515$. (c) $P(\bar{x} < \frac{100}{52}) = P(Z < -1.4267) = 0.0768$.

9.38 (a) $P(Z < -1.5) = 0.0668$. (b) $P(Z < -3) = 0.0013$.

9.39 $\mu + 2.33\sigma/\sqrt{n} = 1.4625$.

9.40 $\mu - 1.645\sigma/\sqrt{n} = 12.513$.

CHAPTER REVIEW

9.41 $P(\hat{p} > 0.50) = P(Z > \frac{0.50-0.45}{0.02225}) = P(Z > 2.247) = 0.01231$.

9.42 (a) $np = (25000)(0.141) = 3525$. (b) $P(X \geq 3500) = P(Z \geq \frac{3500-3525}{55.027}) = P(Z \geq -0.4543) = 0.6752$.

9.43 (a) $P(Z > \frac{105-100}{15}) = P(Z > \frac{1}{3}) = 0.36944$. (b) Mean: 100; standard deviation: 1.93649. (c) $P(Z > \frac{105-100}{1.93649}) = P(Z > 2.5820) = 0.00491$. (d) The answer to (a) could be quite different; (b) would be the same (it does not depend on normality at all). The answer we gave for (c) would be still be fairly reliable because of the central limit theorem.

9.44 $P(\frac{750}{12} < \bar{x} < \frac{825}{12}) = P(-1.732 < Z < 2.598) = 0.95368$.

9.45 (a) No — a count assumes only whole-number values, so it cannot be normally distributed. (b) $N(1.5, 0.02835)$. (c) $P(\bar{x} > \frac{1075}{700}) = P(Z > 1.2599) = 0.10386$.

9.46 (a) $\mu = np = 50$, $\sigma = \sqrt{np(1-p)} = \sqrt{40} = 6.3246$. (b) $P(X \geq 60) = P(Z \geq 1.5811) = 0.0569$ (or find $P(\hat{p} \geq 0.24)$, using the fact that the mean of $\hat{p}$ is 0.2 and the standard deviation is 0.0253 — the computation comes out the same after standardizing). For reference, the "exact" probability is 0.06885.

9.47 $P(5067 \text{ or more heads}) = P(\hat{p} \geq 0.5067) = P(Z \geq 1.34) = 0.0901$. If Kerrich's coin was "fair," we would see 5067 or more heads in about 9% of all repetitions of the experiment of flipping the coin 10,000 times, or about once every 11 attempts. This is *some* evidence against the coin being fair, but it is not by any means overwhelming.

Introduction to Inference

SECTION 10.1

10.1 (a) 44% to 50%. (b) We do not have information about the whole population; we only know about a small sample. We expect our sample to give us a good estimate of the population value, but it will not be exactly correct. (c) The procedure used gives an estimate within 3 percentage points of the true value in 95% of all samples.

10.2 This is a statement about the *mean* score for all young men, not about individual scores. We are only attempting to estimate the center of the population distribution; the scores for individuals are much more variable. Also, "95%" is not a probability or a proportion; it is a confidence level.

10.3 (a) Mean: 280; standard deviation: 1.89737. (b) Below. (c) 2 standard deviations — 3.8 points. (d) Below; the confidence intervals drawn may vary, of course. (e) 95%.

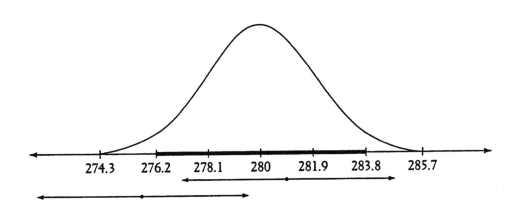

10.4 (a) $N(\mu, 0.05657)$. (b) See the sketch above. For this problem, the "numbers" below the axis would be $\mu - 0.16971$, $\mu - 0.11314$, $\mu - 0.05657$, μ, etc. (c) $m = 0.11314$ (2 standard deviations). (d) 95%. (e) See above.

10.5 11.78 ± 0.77, or 11.01 to 12.55 years.

10.6 (a) The stemplot is *somewhat* normal in appearance — not overwhelmingly so, but reasonably close. (b) 35.091 ± 4.272, or 30.819 to 39.363. (c) We base our confidence interval on the assumption that we have an SRS from the population. If all the students are in the same class, our methods are not reliable — that class might not be representative of the population of all third-graders in the district.

```
1 | 44
1 | 5899
2 | 2
2 | 55667789
3 | 13344
3 | 555589
4 | 0011234
4 | 5667789
5 | 1224
```

10.7 (a) The distribution is slightly skewed to the right. (b) 224.002 ± 0.029, or 223.973 to 224.031.

```
2239 | 01
2239 | 66788889
2240 | 01
2240 | 589
2241 | 2
```

10.8 (a) 3.2 ± 0.329, or 2.871 to 3.529. (b) 3.2 ± 0.190, or 3.010 to 3.390.

10.9 (a) 0.8354 to 0.8454. (b) 0.8275 to 0.8533. (c) Below — increasing confidence makes the interval longer.

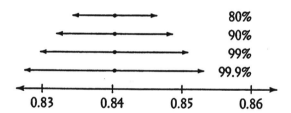

10.10 0.00506 — which is half the margin of error with $n = 3$.

10.11 (a) 271.4 to 278.6. (b) 90%: 272.0 to 278.0; 99%: 270.3 to 279.7. (c) 90%: 3.0; 95%: 3.6; 99%: 4.7. Margin of error goes up with increasing confidence.

10.12 (a) 271.4 to 278.6. (b) 267.6 to 282.4. (c) 273.1 to 276.9. (d) 250: 7.4; 1077: 3.6; 4000: 1.9. Margin of error decreases with larger samples (by a factor of $\sqrt{n}$).

10.13 (a) 10.00209 to 10.00251. (b) 22 (21.64).

10.14 68 (67.95).

10.15 35 (34.57).

10.16 (a) The computations are correct. (b) Since the numbers are based on a voluntary response, rather than an SRS, the methods of this section cannot be used — the interval does not apply to the whole population.

10.17 (a) The interval was based on a method that gives correct results 95% of the time. (b) Since the margin of error was 2%, the true value of p could be as low as 49%. The confidence interval thus contains some values of p which give the election to Ford. (c) The proportion of voters that favor Carter is not random — either a majority favors Carter, or they don't. Discussing probabilities about this proportion has little meaning; the "probability" the politician asked about is either 1 or 0 (respectively).

10.18 (a) We can be 99% confident that between 63% and 69% of all adults favor such an amendment. We estimate the standard deviation of the distribution of $\hat{p}$ to be about $\sqrt{(0.66)(0.34)/1664} = 0.01161$;

dividing 0.03 (the margin of error) by this gives $z^* = 2.58$, the critical value for a 99% confidence interval. (b) The survey excludes people without telephones (a large percentage of whom would be poor), so this group would be underrepresented. Also, Alaska and Hawaii are not included in the sample.

10.19 1.888 to 2.372.

10.20 (a) The intended population is hotel managers (perhaps specifically managers of hotels of the particular size range mentioned). However, because the sample came entirely from Chicago and Detroit, it may not do a good job of representing that larger population. There is also the problem of voluntary response. (b) 5.101 to 5.691. (c) 4.010 to 4.786. (d) We have a large enough sample size that the central limit theorem applies (if we accept the sample as an SRS).

10.21 (a) The intended population is "the American public"; the population which was actually sampled was "citizens of Indianapolis (with listed phone numbers)." (b) Food stores: 15.22 to 22.12; Mass merchandisers: 27.77 to 36.99; Pharmacies: 43.68 to 53.52. (c) The confidence intervals do not overlap at all; in particular, the *lower* confidence limit of the rating for pharmacies is higher than the *upper* confidence limit for the other stores. This indicates that the pharmacies are *really* higher.

10.22 $23,014 to $23,892.

10.23 505 residents.

10.24 The sample size for women was more than twice as large as that for men. Larger sample sizes lead to smaller margins of error (with the same confidence level).

10.25 $657.14 to $670.86. (The sample size is not used; the standard deviation given is $\sigma_{estimate}$).

10.26 (a)

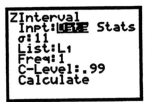 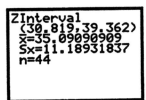

The 99% confidence interval for the mean DRP score is (30.82, 39.36).

(b)

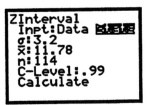 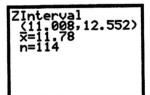

The 99% confidence interval for the mean number of years for the hotel managers is (11.01, 12.55).

SECTION 10.2

10.27 (a) N(115, 6). (b) The actual result lies out toward the high tail of the curve, while 118.6 is fairly close to the middle. Assuming H_0 is true, observing a value like 118.6 would not be surprising, but 125.7 is less likely, and therefore provides evidence against H_0. (c) See page 119.

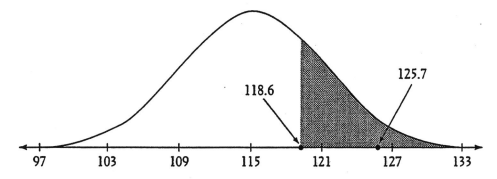

10.28 (a) N(31%, 1.518%). (b) The lower percentage lies out in the low tail of the curve, while 30.2% is fairly close to the middle. Assuming H_0 is true, observing a value like 30.2% would not be surprising, but 27.6% is unlikely, and therefore provides evidence against H_0. (c) Below.

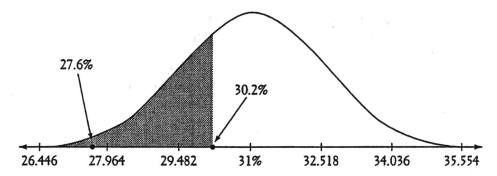

10.29 H_0: $\mu = 5$ mm; H_a: $\mu \neq 5$ mm.

10.30 H_0: $\mu = \$42{,}500$; H_a: $\mu > \$42{,}500$.

10.31 H_0: $\mu = 50$; H_a: $\mu < 50$.

10.32 H_0: $\mu = 2.6$; H_a: $\mu \neq 2.6$.

10.33 The P-values are 0.2743 and 0.0373, respectively.

10.34 The P-values are 0.2991 and 0.0125, respectively.

10.35 (a) $\bar{x} = 398$. (b) A N(354, 19.053) density (below). (c) 0.0105. (d) It is significant at $\alpha = 0.05$, but not at $\alpha = 0.01$. This is pretty convincing evidence against H_0.

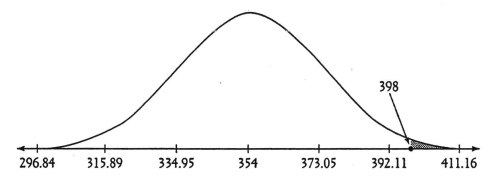

10.36 (a) A N(0, 5.3932) density (see page 120). (b) 0.1004. (c) Not significant at $\alpha = 0.05$. The study gives *some* evidence of increased compensation, but it is not very strong — it would happen 10% of the time just by chance.

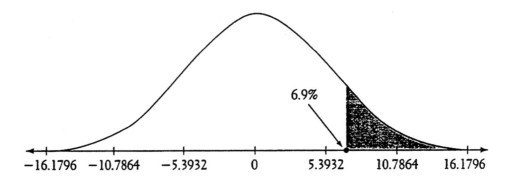

10.37 If church attenders are no more ethnocentric than nonattenders, then the outcomes observed for *this* sample would occur in less than 1 out of 20 instances. This being unlikely, we conclude that church-goers are more ethnocentric.

10.38 Comparing men's and women's earnings for our sample, we observe a difference so large that it would only occur in 3.8% of all samples if men and women actually earned the same amount. Based on this, we conclude that men earn more.

   While there is almost certainly *some* difference between earnings of black and white students in our sample, it is relatively small — if blacks and whites actually earn the same amount, we would still observe a difference as big as what we saw almost half (47.6%) of the time.

10.39 (a) H_0: $\mu = 224$ vs. H_a: $\mu \neq 224$. (b) $z = 0.1292$. (c) $P = 0.8972$ — this is reasonable variation when the null hypothesis is true, so we do not reject H_0.

10.40 (a) H_0: $\mu = 300$ vs. H_a: $\mu < 300$. (b) $z = -0.7893$. (c) $P = 0.2150$ — this is reasonable variation when the null hypothesis is true, so we do not reject H_0.

10.41 (a) $z = -2.200$. (b) Yes, because $|z| > 1.960$. (c) No, because $|z| < 2.576$.

10.42 (a) The command rand(100) $\rightarrow$ L$_1$ generates 100 random numbers in the interval (0,1) and stores them in list L$_1$. Here's a histogram of our simulation: and the 1-variable statistics (your results will be slightly different):

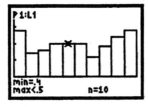
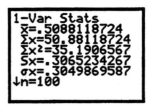

The z test statistic is $z = .3048$, and the P-value is 0.76. We fail to reject H_0.

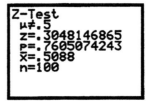

There is no evidence to suggest that the mean of the random numbers generated is different from 0.5.

10.43 (a) Yes, because $z > 1.645$. (b) Yes, because $z > 2.326$.

10.44 (a) 99.86 to 108.40. (b) Because 105 falls in this 90% confidence interval, we cannot reject H_0: $\mu = 105$ in favor of H_a: $\mu \neq 105$.

10.45 (a) $N(0, 0.11339)$ (below). (b) $\bar{x} = 0.27$ lies out in the tail of the curve, while 0.09 is fairly close to the middle. Assuming H_0 is true, observing a value like 0.09 would not be surprising, but 0.27 is unlikely, and therefore provides evidence against H_0. (c) $P = 0.4274$ (the shaded region below). (d) $P = 0.0173$.

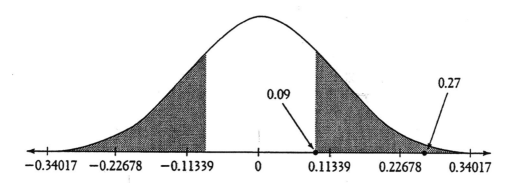

10.46 H_0: $\mu = 1250$ vs. H_a: $\mu < 1250$.

10.47 H_0: $\mu = 18$ vs. H_a: $\mu < 18$.

10.48 Hypotheses: H_0: $\mu = -0.545$ vs. H_a: $\mu > -0.545$. Test statistic: $z = 1.957$. P-value: $P = 0.0252$. We conclude that the mean freezing point really is higher, and thus the supplier *is* apparently adding water.

10.49 (a) No, because $|z| < 1.960$. (b) No, because $|z| < 1.645$.

10.50 P is between 0.02 and 0.04 (in fact, $P = 0.0278$).

10.51 P is between 0.005 and 0.01 (in fact, $P = 0.0078$).

10.52 P is between 0.10 and 0.20 (in fact, $P = 0.1707$).

10.53 $P = 0.1292$. Although this sample showed *some* difference in market share between pioneers with patents or trade secrets and those without, the difference was small enough that it could have arisen merely by chance. The observed difference would occur in about 13% of all samples even if there is *no* difference between the two types of pioneer companies.

10.54 If there were no differences between brands, then what was observed in this particular sample occurs less than once in 1000 times. Since this is so unlikely, we conclude that perceived age does differ between brands. While only a sample of advertisements was used for this study, if it was a randomly chosen sample, it should be a fair representation of *all* ads for these brands.

10.55 When a test is significant at the 1% level, it means that if the null hypothesis is true, outcomes similar to those seen are expected to occur less than once in 100 repetitions of the experiment or sampling. "Significant at the 5% level" means we have observed something which occurs in less than 5 out of 100 repetitions (when H_0 is true). Something that occurs "less than once in 100 repetitions" also occurs "less than 5 times in 100 repetitions," so significance at the 1% level implies significance at the 5% level (or any higher level).

10.56 The explanation is not correct; either H_0 is true (in which case the "probability" that H_0 is true equals 1) or H_0 is false (in which case this "probability" is 0). "Statistically significant at the $\alpha = 0.05$ level" means that *if* H_0 is true, we have observed outcomes that occur less than 5% of the time.

10.57 (a) In Example 10.14, H_0: $\mu_0 = 0.86$, H_a: $\mu \neq 0.86$, and $\sigma = .0068$. Specifying a z test and entering .8404 for the sample mean, the TI-83 screens that specify the information and present the results of the test are shown on page 122. We specified "Calculate."

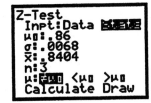

The results, $Z = -4.99$ and P-value $= 5.97 \times 10^{-7} = .0000$, agree with the results in Example 10.14.

(b) $H_0: \mu_0 = 224$, $H_a: \mu \neq 224$, and $\sigma = .060$. Entering the data into list L_1 and specifying a z test, here are the TI-83 screens that specify the information and present the results of the test. We specified "Calculate."

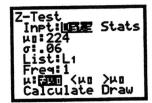
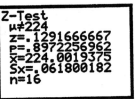

The test statistic is $z = 0.129$, and the P-value is 0.897. Since the P-value is large, there is no evidence that the process mean μ is not equal to the target $\mu_0 = 224$.

(c) $H_0: \mu_0 = 300$, $H_a: \mu < 300$, and $\sigma = 3$. Entering the data into list L_1 and specifying a z test, here are the TI-83 screens that specify the information and present the results of the test. Again, we specified "Calculate."

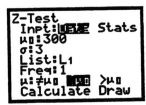
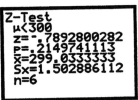

The test statistic is $z = -.789$, and the P-value is 0.215. There is insufficient evidence to conclude that the mean contents of cola bottles is less than 300.

SECTION 10.3

10.58 (a) $z = 1.64$; not significant at 5% level ($P = 0.0505$). (b) $z = 1.65$; significant at 5% level ($P = 0.0495$).

10.59 (a) $P = 0.3821$. (b) $P = 0.1714$. (c) $P = 0.0014$.

10.60 $n = 100$: 452.24 to 503.76. $n = 1,000$: 469.85 to 486.15. $n = 10,000$: 475.42 to 480.58.

10.61 No — the percentage was based on a voluntary response sample, and so cannot be assumed to be a fair representation of the population. Such a poll is likely to draw a higher-than-actual proportion of people with a strong opinion, esp. a strong negative opinion.

10.62 (a) No — in a sample of size 500, we expect to see about 5 people who have a "P-value" of 0.01 or less. These four *might* have ESP, or they may simply be among the "lucky" ones we expect to see. (b) The researcher should repeat the procedure on these four to see if they again perform well.

10.63 A test of significance answers question (b).

10.64 We might conclude that customers prefer design A, but perhaps not "strongly." Because the sample size is so large, this statistically significant difference may not be of any practical importance.

10.65 (a) 0.05. (b) Out of 77 tests, we can expect to see about 3 or 4 (3.85, to be precise) significant tests at the 5% level.

SECTION 10.4

10.66 (a) H_0: the patient is ill (or "the patient should see a doctor"); H_a: the patient is healthy (or "the patient should not see a doctor"). A Type I error means a false negative — clearing a patient who should be referred to a doctor. A Type II error is a false positive — sending a healthy patient to the doctor. (b) One might wish to lower the probability of a false negative so that most ill patients are treated. On the other hand, if money is an issue, or there is concern about sending too many patients to see the doctor, lowering the probability of false positives might be desirable.

10.67 (a) Reject H_0 if $z < -2.326$. (b) 0.01 (the significance level). (c) We accept H_0 if $\bar{x} \geq 270.185$, so when $\mu = 270$, $P(\text{Type II error}) = P(\bar{x} \geq 270.185) = P(\frac{\bar{x} - 270}{60/\sqrt{840}} \geq \frac{270.185 - 270}{60/\sqrt{840}}) = 0.4644$.

10.68 (a) 0.50. (b) 0.1841. (c) 0.0013.

10.69 (a) Reject H_0 if $\bar{x} \geq 0.5202$. (b) 0.9666.

10.70 (a) Reject H_0 if $\bar{x} \leq 297.985$, so the power against $\mu = 299$ is 0.2037. (b) The power against $\mu = 295$ is 0.9926. (c) The power against $\mu = 290$ would be greater — it is further from μ_0 (300), so it is easier to distinguish from the null hypothesis.

10.71 (a) 0.5086. (b) 0.9543.

10.72 (a) Reject if $\bar{x} \geq 0.87011$ or $\bar{x} \leq 0.84989$. (b) Power: 0.89353. (c) $1 - 0.89353 = 0.10647$.

10.73 (a) We reject H_0 if $\bar{x} \geq 131.46$ or $\bar{x} \leq 124.54$. Power: 0.9246. (b) Power: 0.9246 (same as (a)). Over 90% of the time, this test will detect a difference of 6 (in either the positive or negative direction). (c) The power would be higher — it is easier to detect greater differences than smaller ones.

10.74 $P(\text{Type I error}) = 0.05$. $P(\text{Type II error}) = 1 - 0.9926 = 0.0074$.

10.75 Power: $1 - 0.4644 = 0.5356$.

10.76 A test having low power may do a good job of not incorrectly rejecting the null hypothesis, but it is likely to accept H_0 even when some alternative is correct, simply because it is difficult to distinguish between H_0 and "nearby" alternatives.

CHAPTER REVIEW

10.77 (a) The plot is reasonably symmetric for such a small sample. (b) 26.06 to 34.74. (c) H_0: $\mu = 25$ vs. H_a: $\mu > 25$; $z = 2.44$; P-value $= .007$. This is strong evidence against H_0.

```
2 | 034
2 |
3 | 01124
3 | 6
4 | 3
```

10.78 (a) 141.6 to 148.4. (b) H_0: $\mu = 140$ vs. H_a: $\mu > 140$; $z = 2.421$; P-value is about 0.0077. This strongly supports H_a over H_0. (c) We must assume that the 15 cuttings in our sample are an SRS. Since our sample is not too large, the population should be normally distributed, or at least not extremely nonnormal.

10.79 12.285 to 13.515. This assumes that the babies are an SRS from the population. The population should not be too nonnormal (although a sample of size 26 will overcome quite a bit of skewness).

10.80 (a) H_0: $\mu = 32$ vs. H_a: $\mu > 32$. (b) $z = 1.8639$; P-value is 0.0312. This is strong evidence against H_0 — observations this extreme would only occur in about 3 out of 100 samples if H_0 were true.

10.81 (a) Narrower; lowering confidence level decreases the interval size. (b) Yes: \$33,000 falls outside the 99% confidence interval, indicating that $P < 0.01$.

10.82 (a) Margin of error decreases. (b) The P-value decreases (the evidence against H_0 becomes stronger). (c) The power increases (the test becomes better at distinguishing between the null and alternative hypotheses).

10.83 H_0: $p = \frac{18}{38}$ vs. H_a: $p \neq \frac{18}{38}$.

10.84 No — "$P = 0.03$" *does* mean that the null hypothesis is unlikely, but only in the sense that the evidence (from the sample) would not occur very often if H_0 were true. P is a probability associated with the sample, not the null hypothesis; H_0 is either true or it isn't.

10.85 Yes — significance tests allow us to discriminate between random differences ("chance variation") that might occur when the null hypothesis is true, and differences that are unlikely to occur when H_0 is true.

10.86 (a) The difference observed in the study would occur in less than 1% of all samples if the two populations actually have the same proportion. (b) The interval is constructed using a method that is correct (i.e., contains the actual proportion) 95% of the time. (c) No — treatments were not randomly assigned, but instead were chosen by the mothers. Mothers who choose to attend a job training program may be more inclined to get themselves out of welfare.

11

Inference for Distributions

SECTION 11.1

11.1 (a) The t_2 curve is a bit shorter at the peak and slightly higher in the tails (see TI-83 plot). (b) The t_9 curve has moved toward coincidence with the standard normal curve. (c) The t_{30} curve cannot be distinguished from the standard normal curve. As the degrees of freedom increase, the t (df) curve approaches the standard normal density graph.

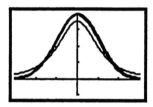

11.2 (a) and (b)

df	$P(t > 2)$	Absolute difference
2	.0917	.0689
10	.0367	.0139
30	.0273	.0045
50	.0255	.0027
100	.0241	.0013

(c) As the degrees of freedom increases, the area to the right of 2 under the t_{df} distribution gets closer to the area under the standard normal curve to the right of 2.

11.3 $37/\sqrt{4} = 18.5$.

11.4 (a) 2.015. (b) 2.518.

11.5 (a) 2.145. (b) 0.688.

11.6 (a) 2.262. (b) 2.861. (c) 1.440.

11.7 (a) 14. (b) 1.82 is between 1.761 ($p = 0.05$) and 2.145 ($p = 0.025$). (c) The P-value is between 0.025 and 0.05 (in fact, $P = 0.0451$). (d) $t = 1.82$ is significant at $\alpha = 0.05$ but not at $\alpha = 0.01$.

11.8 (a) 24. (b) 1.12 is between 1.059 ($p = 0.15$) and 1.318 ($p = 0.10$). (c) The P-value is between 0.30 and 0.20 (in fact, $P = 0.2738$). (d) $t = 1.12$ is not significant at either $\alpha = 0.10$ or at $\alpha = 0.05$.

11.9 (a) $\bar{x} = 1.75$ and $s = 0.1291$, so $SE(\bar{x}) = 0.06455$. (b) 1.598 to 1.902.

11.10 (a) $\bar{x} = 5.36667$ and $SE(\bar{x}) = 0.27162$. (b) 4.819 to 5.914.

11.11 H_0: $\mu = 1.3$ vs. H_a: $\mu > 1.3$; $t = 6.9714$; the P-value is between 0.005 and 0.0025 (in fact, $P = 0.003$). This is very strong evidence against the null; we conclude that DDT does slow nerve recovery.

11.12 (a) μ is the difference between the population mean yields for Variety A plants and Variety B plants; that is, $\mu = \mu_A - \mu_B$. Another (equivalent) description is: μ is the mean difference between Variety A yields and Variety B yields. (b) H_0: $\mu = 0$ vs. H_a: $\mu > 0$. (c) $t = 1.295$, $P = 0.1137$. This is not enough evidence to reject H_0 — the difference could be due to chance variation.

11.13 (a) Randomly assign 12 (or 13) into a group which will use the right-hand knob first; the rest should use the left-hand knob first. Alternatively, for each student, randomly select which knob he or she should use first. (b) μ is the difference between right-handed times and left-handed times; the null hypothesis is H_0: $\mu = 0$ (no difference). How the alternative is written depends on exactly how μ is defined. Let μ_R be the mean right-hand thread time for all right-handed people (or students), and μ_L be the mean left-hand thread time. As described above, we would most naturally write $\mu = \mu_R - \mu_L$; in this case, H_a: $\mu < 0$. Alternatively, we might define $\mu = \mu_L - \mu_R$, so that H_a: $\mu > 0$. Either way, the null hypothesis says $\mu_R = \mu_L$ and the alternative is $\mu_R < \mu_L$. (c) $\bar{x} = -13.32$ (or $+13.32$), $SE(\bar{x}) = 4.5872$, $t = \pm 2.9037$, and $P = 0.0039$. We reject H_0 in favor of H_a.

11.14 5.47 to 21.17 seconds. For our sample $\bar{x}_R \div \bar{x}_L = 88.7\%$; this suggests that right-handed students working on an assembly line with right-handed threads would complete their task in about 90% of the time that it would take them to complete the same task with left-handed threads.

11.15 (a) 1.54 to 1.80. (b) We are told the distribution is symmetric; because the scores range from 1 to 5, there is a limit to how much skewness there might be. In this situation, the assumption that the 17 Mexicans are an SRS from the population is the most crucial.

11.16 (a) H_0: $\mu = 0$ vs. H_a: $\mu > 0$. $t = 43.5$; the P-value is basically 0, so we reject H_0 and conclude that the new policy would increase credit card usage. (b) $312 to $352. (c) The sample size is very large, and we are told that we have an SRS. This means that outliers are the only potential snag, and there are none. (d) Make the offer to an SRS of 200 customers, and choose another SRS of 200 as a control group. Compare the mean increase for the two groups.

11.17 (a) The distribution is slightly skewed, but there are no apparent outliers. (b) H_0: $\mu = 224$ vs. H_a: $\mu \neq 224$. $t = 0.12536$ and $P = 0.9019$, so we have very little evidence against H_0.

```
2239 | 01
2239 | 6688899
2240 | 002
2240 | 69
2241 | 02
```

11.18 (a) On page 127. (b) H_0: $\mu = 105$ vs. H_a: $\mu \neq 105$, $t = -0.3195$, $P = 0.7554$. We do not reject the null hypothesis — the mean detector reading could be 105.

```
 9 | 2
 9 | 578
10 | 024
10 | 55
11 | 1
11 | 9
12 | 2
```

11.19 (a) Approximately 2.403 (from Table C), or 2.405 (using software). (b) Using $t^* = 2.403$: Reject H_0 if $t > 2.403$, which means $\bar{x} > 36.70$. (c) The power against $\mu = 100$ is 0.99998—basically 1. A sample of size 50 should be quite adequate.

11.20 (a) The power is 0.5287. (Reject H_0 if $t > 1.833$, i.e., if $\bar{x} > 0.4811$.) (b) The power is 0.9034. (Reject H_0 if $t > 1.711$, i.e., if $\bar{x} > 0.2840$.)

11.21 (a) 9. (b) $P = 0.0255$; it lies between 0.05 and 0.025.

11.22 (a) 21.47 to 26.53. (b) The sample is large enough that deviations from the assumptions do not greatly affect the validity of the t test.

11.23 (a) 111.22 to 118.58. (b) We assume that the 27 members of the placebo group can be viewed as an SRS of the population, and that the distribution of seated systolic BP in this population is normal, or at least not too nonnormal. Since the sample size is somewhat large, the procedure should be valid as long as the data show no outliers and no strong skewness.

11.24 $\bar{x} = 22.125$. The standard error of $\bar{x}$ is 1.0451; the margin of error depends on the confidence level—two possible answers are ± 3.326 (if $C = 95\%$) and ± 6.105 (if $C = 99\%$). A margin of error of ± 3.326 means that we are 95% confident—that is, we have used a procedure that is correct 95% of the time—that the actual mean is between 18.799 and 25.451.

11.25 (a) Standard error of the mean (b) $s = 0.01\sqrt{3} = 0.01732$. (c) 0.84 ± 0.0292; i.e., 0.8108 to 0.8692.

11.26 (a) H_0: $\mu = 0$ vs. H_a: $\mu > 0$, where μ is the population mean of post-test minus pre-test scores. (b) Stemplot (below) shows no outliers, with a slight skewness to the left, but nothing too strong. (c) $\bar{x} = 1.45$, $SE(\bar{x}) = 0.71626$, and $t = 2.0244$; the P-value equals 0.029. This is significant at the 5% level, but not at 1%. (d) 0.2116 to 2.6884.

```
−0 | 54
−0 | 32
−0 | 11
 0 | 11
 0 | 2223333
 0 | 4455
 0 | 7
```

11.27 (a) H_0: $\mu = 0$ vs. H_a: $\mu \neq 0$. For each subject, randomly choose which test to administer first. Alternatively, randomly assign 11 subjects to the "ARSMA first" group, and the rest to the "BI first" group. (b) $t = 4.27$; the P-value is less than 0.001, so we reject H_0. (c) 0.1292 to 0.3746.

11.28 (a) The sample size is large enough that skewness (in the absence of outliers) has little effect on our procedures. (b) df = 103. (c) 2.419 to 11.381; the data must be an SRS from the population of all corporate CEOs.

11.29 We know the data for *all* presidents; we know about the whole population, not just a sample. (We might want to try to make statements about future presidents, but doing so from this data would be highly questionable; they can hardly be considered an SRS from the population.)

11.30 (a) 2.080. (b) Reject H_0 if $|t| \geq 2.080$, i.e., if $|\bar{x}| \geq 0.133$. (c) $P(|\bar{x}| \geq 0.133) = P(\bar{x} \leq -0.133$ or $\bar{x} \geq 0.133) = P(Z \leq -5.207$ or $Z \geq -1.047) = 0.852$.

SECTION 11.2

11.31 (a) (3) — two samples. (b) (2) — matched pairs.

11.32 (a) (1) — single sample. (b) (3) — two samples.

11.33 (a) H_0: $\mu_1 = \mu_2$ vs. H_a: $\mu_1 < \mu_2$, where μ_1 is the beta-blocker population mean pulse rate and μ_2 is the placebo mean pulse rate. $t = -2.4525$; use a $t(29)$ distribution, which gives $P = 0.01022$. This makes the result significant at 5% but not at 1%. (b) -10.8311 to 0.6311.

11.34 H_0: $\mu_1 = \mu_2$ vs. H_a: $\mu_1 > \mu_2$, where μ_1 and μ_2 are the mean number of beetles on untreated (control) plots and malathion-treated plots, respectively. $t = 5.8090$, which yields $P < 0.0001$ for a $t(12)$ distribution — this is significant at the 1% level.

11.35 (a) If k (the degrees of freedom) is reasonably large, the $t(k)$ distribution looks enough like the $N(0, 1)$ distribution that for $t = 7.36$, we can conclude that the P-value is tiny (based on the 68-95-99.7 rule), so the result is significant. (b) Use a $t(32)$ distribution.

11.37 (a) Because the sample sizes are so large (and the sample sizes are almost the same), deviation from the assumptions have little effect. (b) Using $t^* = 1.660$ from a $t(100)$ distribution, the interval is $412.68 to $635.58. Using $t^* = 1.6473$ from a $t(620)$ distribution (obtained with software), the interval is $413.54 to $634.72. (c) The sample is not *really* random, but there is no reason to expect that the method used should introduce any bias into the sample. (d) Students without employment were excluded, so the survey results can only (possibly) extend to *employed* undergraduates. Knowing the number of unreturned questionnaires would also be useful.

11.38 (a) Both stemplots show no outliers; the experimental data (on the right side) is perhaps slightly skewed, but not enough to keep us from using the t procedures. (b) H_0: $\mu_1 = \mu_2$ vs. H_a: $\mu_1 < \mu_2$ ($\mu_1 =$ control weight gain, ...). $\bar{x}_1 = 366.30$, $s_1 = 50.8052$, $\bar{x}_2 = 402.95$, $s_2 = 42.7286$, and $t = -2.469$; this gives $P = 0.0116$ (for a $t(19)$ distribution), so we reject H_0. (c) 5.58 to 67.72 grams.

87	2	
322	3	234
887666555	3	6899
3100	4	0011123333
66	4	578

11.39 (a) Women are on the left side; men on the right. Both distributions are slightly skewed to the right, and have one or two moderate high outliers. A t procedure may be (cautiously) used nonetheless, since the sum of the sample sizes is almost 40. (b) H_0: $\mu_w = \mu_m$ vs. H_a: $\mu_w > \mu_m$. $\bar{x}_w = 141.056$, $s_w = 26.4363$, $\bar{x}_m = 121.250$, $s_m = 32.8519$, and $t = 2.0561$, so $P = 0.0277$ (for a $t(17)$ distribution). (c) For $\mu_m - \mu_w$: -36.57 to -3.05.

```
        7 | 05
        8 | 8
        9 | 12
  931  10 | 489
    5  11 | 3455
  966  12 | 6
   77  13 | 2
   80  14 | 06
  442  15 | 1
   55  16 | 9
    8  17 |
       18 | 07
       19 |
    0  20 |
```

11.40 Consider the left and right endpoint of the confidence interval. If these endpoints remain fixed, then as the degrees of freedom increase, the area in the tails (outside the confidence interval and under the t_{df} curve) decreases. See Exercise 11.1. To make up this difference in area, the endpoints of the intervals have to move toward the center of the distribution, giving up some area to the tails. Thus the confidence interval becomes narrower.

11.41 Here are the key calculator screens.

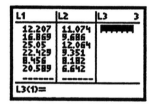  

The test statistic is $t = 2.99$. With df $= 5.9376$, the P-value is .0246.

11.43 (a) H_0: $\mu_{skilled} = \mu_{novice}$ vs. H_a: $\mu_s > \mu_n$. (b) The t statistic we want is the "Unequal" value: $t = 3.1583$; its P-value is 0.0052. This is strong evidence against H_0. (c) Using $t^* = 1.833$ from a $t(9)$ distribution: 0.4922 to 1.8535. Using $t^* = 1.8162$ from a $t(9.8)$ distribution (from software): 0.4984 to 1.8473.

11.44 H_0: $\mu_{skilled} = \mu_{novice}$ vs. H_a: $\mu_s \neq \mu_n$ (use a two-sided alternative since we have no preconceived idea of the direction of the difference). The t statistic we want is $t = 0.5143$; its P-value is 0.6165. There is no significant difference in weight between skilled and novice rowers.

11.45 Conservative: 19882 d.f.; more exact method: 38786 d.f. Either way, the distribution we use is almost exactly a $N(0, 1)$ distribution. To three decimal places, $t^* = 2.576$, so the confidence interval is 27.91 to 32.09. Normality of SAT scores is not necessary since the sample sizes are so large.

11.46 (a) H_0: $\mu_{breast-fed} = \mu_{formula}$ vs. H_a: $\mu_{bf} \neq \mu_f$ (the question implies no preconceived idea of the direction of the difference). Conservative: 18 d.f.; more exact method: 37.6 d.f. $t = 1.654$; the conservative P-value is 0.1155, and the more exact P-value is 0.1065; in either case, the results are not significant at the 10% level. (b) $t(18)$: $t^* = 2.101$; -0.2434 to 2.0434. $t(37.6)$: $t^* = 2.0251$; -0.2021 to 2.0021. (c) We assume that both groups are SRSs of mothers of both types, and that both distributions are normal — or at least don't depart too much from normality, and have no outliers. (d) This is not an experiment — the mothers chose the feeding method. This may confound the conclusions, since there may have been other factors that affected this choice.

11.47 (a) H_0: $\mu_1 = \mu_2$ vs. H_a: $\mu_1 \neq \mu_2$. $t = -8.2379$; using either a $t(13)$ or a $t(21.8)$ distribution, the P-value is smaller than 0.0001, so there is a significant difference. (b) The fact that all the subjects in this study are college professors may have some confounding effects on the results. Additionally, all the subjects volunteered for a fitness program, which could bring in some further confounding.

11.48 (a) Use either a $t(52)$ or a $t(121.9)$ distribution. For the former, the nearest table value is $t^* = 2.009$, and the interval is -1.279 to 7.279. For 121.9 d. f., the interval is -1.216 to 7.216. (b) The samples taken by the market research firm do not give complete information about *all* stores. When we allow for the possible variation that might reasonably occur at the stores not included in the samples, we find that the actual sales might have dropped by 1.3 units, or could have risen by as much as 7.3 units.

11.49 (a) H_0: $\mu_A = \mu_B$ vs. H_a: $\mu_A \neq \mu_B$; $t = -1.484$. Using $t(149)$ and $t(297.2)$ distributions, P equals 0.1399 and 0.1388, respectively; not significant in either case. The bank might choose to implement Proposal A even though the difference is not significant, since it may have a *slight* advantage over Proposal B. Otherwise, the bank should choose whichever option costs them less. (b) Because the sample sizes are equal and large, the t procedure is reliable in spite of the skewness. (c) This is an experiment — treatments are imposed by the bank. However, one other thing might be useful: statistics for a control group, to see if either plan increased spending.

11.50 (a) Stemplots show little skewness, but one moderate outlier (85) for the control group on the right. Nonetheless, the t procedures should be fairly reliable since the total sample size is 44. (b) H_0: $\mu_t = \mu_c$ vs. H_a: $\mu_t < \mu_c$; $t = 2.311$. Using $t(20)$ and $t(37.9)$ distributions, P equals 0.0158 and 0.0132, respectively; reject H_0. (c) Randomization was not really possible, because existing classes were used — the researcher could not shuffle the students around.

	1	079
4	2	068
3	3	377
9964333	4	1222368
98776432	5	3455
721	6	02
1	7	
	8	5

11.51 (a) H_0: $\mu_c = \mu_a$ vs. H_a: $\mu_c \neq \mu_a$; $t = 1.249$. Using $t(9)$ and $t(25.4)$ distributions, P equals 0.2431 and 0.2229, respectively; the difference is not significant. (b) -15.8 to 54.8 (using $t(9)$) or -12.6 to 51.6 (using $t(25.4)$). These intervals had to contain 0 because according to (a), the observed difference would occur in more than 22% of samples when the means are the same; thus 0 would appear in any confidence interval with a confidence level greater than 78%.

11.52 If they did (for example) 20 tests at the 5% level of significance, they might see 1 or 2 significant differences even when all null hypotheses are true.

11.53 (a) $t^* = 2.364$, the value for a $t(100)$ distribution (since values for a $t(99)$ distribution are not given). (b) Reject H_0 when $\bar{x}_1 - \bar{x}_2 \geq 2.6746$. (c) Power: $P(Z \geq -2.0554) = 0.9801$.

11.54 (a) H_0: $\mu_1 = \mu_2$ vs. H_a: $\mu_1 \neq \mu_2$; $t = (\bar{x}_1 - \bar{x}_2)/\sqrt{\dfrac{s_1^2}{n_1} + \dfrac{s_2^2}{n_2}}$. (b) $t^* = 1.984$, from a $t(100)$ distribution. (c) Reject H_0 when $|\bar{x}_1 - \bar{x}_2| \geq 8.260$; power against $\mu_1 - \mu_2 = 10$: $P[(\bar{x}_1 - \bar{x}_2) \leq -8.260$ or $(\bar{x}_1 - \bar{x}_2) \geq 8.260] = P(Z \leq -4.386$ or $Z \geq -0.4179) = 0.662$.

11.55 (a) H_0: $\mu_A = \mu_B$ vs. H_a: $\mu_A \neq \mu_B$; $t = (\bar{x}_A - \bar{x}_B)/\sqrt{\dfrac{s_A^2}{n_A} + \dfrac{s_B^2}{n_B}}$. (b) For a $t(349)$ distribution, $t^* = 1.967$; using a $t(100)$ distribution, take $t^* = 1.984$. (c) We reject H_0 when $|\bar{x}_A - \bar{x}_B| \geq 59.48$ (using $t^* = 1.967$). To find the power against $|\mu_A - \mu_B| = 100$, we choose *either* $\mu_A - \mu_B = 100$ or $\mu_A - \mu_B = -100$ (the probability is the same either way). Taking the former, we compute: $P[(\bar{x}_A - \bar{x}_B) \leq -59.48$ or $(\bar{x}_A - \bar{x}_B) \geq 59.48] = P(Z \leq -5.274$ or $Z \geq -1.340) = 0.9099$. Repeating these computations with $t^* = 1.984$ gives power 0.9071.

CHAPTER REVIEW

11.56 (a) The observations are "before-and-after" weights, so the pairs of observations will be highly correlated — it is the change in weight that we are interested in. (b) We expect some variation in the weight change, and there may have been some loss due to chance, but the amount lost was so great that it is unlikely to occur merely by chance. In short, this weight-loss program seems to work. (c) Table C shows that the P-value must be smaller than 0.0005; in fact, it is less than 0.00002.

11.57 (a) This is a two-sample t test — the two groups of women are (presumably) independent. (b) Use a $t(44)$ distribution. (c) The sample sizes are large enough that nonnormality has little effect on the reliability of the procedure.

11.58 (a) Using a $t(1361)$ distribution, you get $1016.56 to $1069.44; using a $t(2669.1)$ distribution, you get almost the same interval: $1016.58 to $1069.42. (b) Skewness will have little effect because the sample sizes are very large.

11.59 (a) H_0: $\mu_1 = \mu_2$ vs. H_a: $\mu_1 < \mu_2$; $t = -8.947$; P-value is basically 0 (however one chooses the degrees of freedom). We reject H_0 and conclude that the workers have higher output. (b) The t procedures are robust against skewness when the sample sizes are large. (c) Insertions for experienced workers have (approximately) a $N(\bar{x}_2, s_2)$ distribution; the 68-95-99.7 rule tells us that 95% of all workers can insert between $\bar{x}_2 - 2s_2 = 29.66$ and $\bar{x}_2 + 2s_2 = 44.99$ pins in the allotted time. (We might also choose $\bar{x}_2 \pm 1.96s_2$, but given the other approximations we are making, $\pm 2s_2$ is quite adequate).

11.60 (a) H_0: $\mu_1 = \mu_2$ vs. H_a: $\mu_1 > \mu_2$. Use a matched-pairs t procedure, since the pairs of scores are related. (b) The stemplot is skewed and not symmetric, and the sample size is not large enough to overcome these violations of the assumptions.

```
-1 | 6
-1 |
-0 | 6555
-0 | 3
 0 | 1234
 0 | 55
```

11.61 Both stemplots are reasonably symmetrical, though the nitrite group (on the right) may be slightly left-skewed. There are no extreme outliers. H_0: $\mu_c = \mu_n$ vs. H_a: $\mu_c > \mu_n$; $t = 0.8909$ and P equals 0.1902 (using a $t(29)$ distribution) or 0.1884 (with 56.8 d.f.). In either case, the difference is not significant.

```
          | 5  | 0
      6   | 5  | 6
          | 6  | 23
      765 | 6  | 5668
    42211 | 7  | 34
     9987 | 7  | 67779
   422111 | 8  | 011233
     8765 | 8  | 56689
    41000 | 9  |
          | 9  | 559
       30 | 10 | 2
```

11.62 (a) The stemplot shows some left-skewness; however, for such a small sample, the data are not unreasonably skewed. There are no outliers. (b) 54.78 to 64.40.

```
   4 | 9
   5 | 1
   5 | 5
   6 | 1334
   6 | 55
```

11.63 (a) The stemplot is reasonably symmetrical given the small sample size. There are no outliers. (b) 903.23 to 912.27. (c) No, because 910 falls inside the 95% confidence interval.

```
   89 | 3
   89 | 57
   90 | 1
   90 | 566678
   91 | 34
   91 | 688
   92 | 1
```

11.64 (a) "s. e." stands for standard error (of the mean). $\bar{x}_1 = 2821$, $s_1 = 435.58$; $\bar{x}_2 = 2844$, $s_2 = 437.30$; $\bar{x}_3 = 0.24$, $s_3 = 0.59397$; $\bar{x}_4 = 0.39$, $s_4 = 1.0021$. (b) No. $t = -0.3532$, and $P = 0.7248$ (using $t(82)$) or 0.7243 (using $t(173.9)$) — in either case, there is little evidence against H_0. (c) Not very significant — $t = -1.1972$, and $P = 0.2346$ (using $t(82)$) or 0.2334 (using $t(128.4)$). (d) 0.207 to 0.573. (e) -0.3119 to 0.0119 (using $t(82)$) or -0.3114 to 0.0114 (using $t(128.4)$).

11.65 No — you have information about all Indiana counties (not just a sample).

11.66 (a) $t = 1.897$, so $P = 0.0326$ — not significant at 1%. (b) Use a matched-pairs design, with each soil specimen split in half and measured by each method. Then test H_0: $\mu_1 = \mu_2$ vs. H_a: $\mu_1 \neq \mu_2$.

11.67 (a) H_0: $\mu_1 = \mu_2$ vs. H_a: $\mu_1 > \mu_2$; $t = 1.1738$, so $P = 0.1265$ (using $t(22)$) or 0.123453 (using $t(43.3)$). Not enough evidence to reject H_0. (b) -14.57 to 52.57, or -13.64 to 51.64. (c) 165.53 to 220.47. (d) We are assuming that we have two SRSs from each population, and that underlying distributions are normal. It is unlikely that we have random samples from either population, especially among pets.

11.68 The stemplot looks fairly good; 48.8 is perhaps a moderate low outlier, but is not too far from the other observations. Our estimate is the mean, $\bar{x} = 5.4479$. The standard error of the mean is 0.0410; the margin of error depends on the confidence level chosen. Here are three possibilities:

Confidence level	Confidence interval	Margin of error
90%	(5.3781, 5.5177)	0.0698
95%	(5.3639, 5.5320)	0.0840
99%	(5.3345, 5.5613)	0.1134

```
48 | 8
49 |
50 | 7
51 | 0
52 | 6799
53 | 04469
54 | 2467
55 | 03578
56 | 12358
57 | 59
58 | 5
```

11.69 Choice of confidence level may vary, of course; using 95% confidence we get: for abdomen skinfold: -15.5 to -11.5 (using $t(19)$), or -15.4 to -11.6 (using $t(103.6)$). For thigh skinfold: -12.95 to -9.65 (using $t(19)$), or -12.86 to -9.74 (using $t(106.4)$).

11.70 We have 30 available observations; the distribution is right-skewed, with a high outlier of 123. A 95% confidence interval for the mean city particulate level is 54.067 ± 7.246, or 46.82 to 61.31. If we discard the outlier, we get 51.69 ± 5.57, or 46.12 to 57.26.

Confidence intervals should be used with caution here — the outlier makes t procedures suspect, and discarding the outlier may cause us to underestimate the actual mean.

```
 2 | 3
 3 | 4899
 4 | 12222455689
 5 | 017789
 6 | 089
 7 | 12
 8 | 26
 9 |
10 |
11 |
12 | 3
```

11.71 The distribution of differences (city minus rural) has 26 observations. There are two high outliers (15 and 18). If we naïvely use the t procedures in spite of the outliers, we get $\bar{x} = 2.192$, $s = 4.691$, and $t = 2.383$; the P-value for testing H_0: $\mu_c = \mu_r$ vs. H_a: $\mu_c > \mu_r$ is 0.0125 — pretty strong evidence against H_0. A 95% confidence interval for $\mu_c - \mu_r$ is 0.297 to 4.087.

If we throw out those outliers, the data seem to be more suitable for a t procedure. Using the other 24 observations, $\bar{x} = 1.00$, $s = 2.1059$, $t = 2.326$, and $P = 0.0146$ — we can still reject H_0, even though we have removed from the data the two strongest individual pieces of evidence against H_0. A 95% confidence interval for $\mu_c - \mu_r$ is 0.111 to 1.889.

```
-0 | 32
-0 | 11110
 0 | 01111111
 0 | 2222222
 0 | 5
 0 | 7
 0 |
 1 |
 1 |
 1 | 5
 1 |
 1 | 8
```

11.72 The plot shows a strong positive linear relationship; there is only one observation — (51,69) — which deviates from the pattern slightly. The regression line $\hat{y} = -2.580 + 1.0935x$ explains $r^2 = 95.1\%$ of the variation in the data. When $x = 88$, we predict $\hat{y} = 93.65$.

The point (108,123) is a potentially influential observation (although it does not seem to deviate from the pattern of the other points). Computing the regression line without this point gives $\hat{y} = 1.963 + 0.9942x$ and $r^2 = 92.1\%$, and $\hat{y} = 89.45$ when $x = 88$.

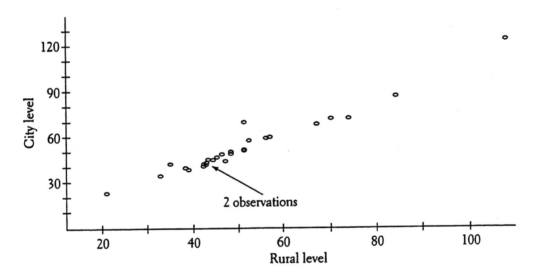

12

Inference for Proportions

SECTION 12.1

12.1 (a) Population: the 175 residents of Tonya's dorm; p is the proportion who like the food. (b) $\hat{p} = 0.28$.

12.2 (a) The population is the 2400 students at Glen's college, and p is the proportion who believe tuition is too high. (b) $\hat{p} = 0.76$.

12.3 (a) The population is the 15,000 alumni, and p is the proportion who support the president's decision. (b) $\hat{p} = 0.38$.

12.4 (a) No — the population is not large enough relative to the sample. (b) Yes — we have an SRS, the population is 48 times as large as the sample, and the success count (38) and failure count (12) are both greater than 10. (c) No — there were only 5 or 6 "successes" in the sample.

12.5 (a) No — np_0 and $n(1 - p_0)$ are less than 10 (they both equal 5). (b) No — the expected number of failures is less than $10 (n(1 - p_0) = 2)$. (c) Yes — we have an SRS, the population is more than 10 times as large as the sample, and $np_0 = n(1 - p_0) = 10$.

12.6 (a) We have an SRS, the population is 50 times as large as the sample, and we observed 86 successes and 14 failures. (b) 0.792 to 0.928.

12.7 $\hat{p} = X/n = 7741/17592 = .44.$ $H_0: p = .40, H_a: p > .40.$ $z = (\hat{p} - p_0)/\sqrt{((.4)(.6)/n))} = 10.84.$ The P-value is .0000. Reject H_0, and conclude that more than 40% of all college students engage in binge drinking.

12.8 (a) 59.4% to 72.6%. (b) $H_0: p = 0.73$ vs. $H_a: p \neq 0.73$; $\hat{p} = 0.66$, $z = -2.23$ and $P = 0.02576$ — reject H_0. (c) We have an SRS; assuming that there are at least 2000 new students, the population is more than 10 times as large as the sample; we observed 132 successes and 68 failures.

12.9 (a) $\hat{p} = 0.5005$, $z = 0.1549$, and $P = 0.8769$ — accept the null hypothesis at any reasonable level of significance. (b) 0.4922 to 0.5088.

12.10 (a) 1051.7 — round up to 1052. (b) 1067.1 — round up to 1068; 16 additional people.

12.11 450.2 — round up to 451.

12.12 This exercise is a follow-up to Activity 12.

12.13

X	n	$\hat{p}$	z	P-value
14	50	.28	$-.752$	.2261
98	350	.28	-1.998	.0233
140	500	.28	-2.378	.0088

Although Tonya, Frank, and Sarah all recorded the same sample proportion, $\hat{p} = .28$, the P-values were all quite different. Conclude: For a given sample proportion, the larger the sample size, the smaller the P-value.

12.14 6.64% to 10.26%.

12.15 $\hat{p} = 0.05227$, $z = -3.337$, and $P < 0.0005$ — very strong evidence against H_0, and in favor of H_a: $p < \frac{1}{10}$.

12.16 (a) 39.0% to 45.0%. (b) Since 50% falls outside the 99% confidence interval, this is strong evidence against H_0: $p = 0.5$ in favor of H_a: $p < 0.5$. (In fact, $z = -6.75$ and P is tiny.) (c) 16589.4 — round up to 16590. The use of $p^* = 0.5$ is reasonable because our confidence interval shows that the actual p is in the range 0.3 to 0.7.

12.17 (a) 0.0913 to 0.2060. (b) 304. (c) The sample comes from a limited area in Indiana, focuses on only one kind of business, and leaves out any businesses not in the Yellow Pages (there might be a few of these; perhaps they are more likely to fail). It is more realistic to believe that this describes businesses that match the above profile; it *might* generalize to food-and-drink establishments elsewhere, but probably not to hardware stores and other types of business.

12.18 (a) H_0: $p = 0.5$ vs. H_a: $p > 0.5$, $z = 1.697$, $P = 0.0448$ — reject H_0 at the 5% level. (b) 0.5071 to 0.7329. (c) The coffee should be presented in random order — some should get the instant coffee first, and others the fresh-brewed first.

12.19 (a) 4719. (b) 0.01125.

12.20 (a)

p	0.1	0.2	0.3	0.4	0.5	0.6	0.7	0.8	0.9
m	.0588	.0784	.0898	.0960	.0980	.0960	.0898	.0784	.0588
(b) m	.0263	.0351	.0402	.0429	.0438	.0429	.0402	.0351	.0263

The new margins of error are less than half their former size (in fact, they have decreased by a factor of $\frac{1}{\sqrt{5}} = 0.447$.)

SECTION 12.2

12.21 (a) -0.0208 to 0.1476. (b) The population-to-sample ratio is certainly large enough, and the smallest count in any category is 75 — much larger than 5.

12.22 (a) 0.0341 to 0.0757. (b) All counts are larger than 5 (the smallest is 54), and the populations are much larger than the samples.

12.23 (a) H_0: $p_1 = p_2$ vs. H_a: $p_1 \neq p_2$. The population-to-sample ratio is large enough, and the smallest number of people in any category is 94 (Catholics answering "Yes"). (b) $\hat{p}_1 = 0.6030$, $\hat{p}_2 = 0.5913$, $\hat{p} = 0.5976$; $z = 0.2650$, and $P = 0.7910$ — H_0 is quite plausible given this sample.

12.24 (a) H_0: $p_1 = p_2$ vs. H_a: $p_1 \neq p_2$; the populations are much larger than the samples, and 44 (the smallest count) is much bigger than 5. (b) $\hat{p} = 0.0933$, $z = -3.802$, and $P < 0.0002$ — the difference is statistically significant.

12.25 (a) H_0: $p_1 = p_2$ vs. H_a: $p_1 > p_2$; the populations are much larger than the samples, and 17 (the smallest count) is greater than 5. (b) $\hat{p} = 0.0632$, $z = 2.926$, and $P = 0.0017$ — the difference is statistically significant. (c) Neither the subjects nor the researchers who had contact with them knew which subjects were getting which drug — if anyone had known, they might confound the outcome by letting their expectations or biases affect the results.

12.26 (a) H_0: $p_1 = p_2$ vs. H_a: $p_1 \neq p_2$; $P = 0.0028$ — the difference is statistically significant. (b) 0.1172 to 0.3919.

12.27 H_0: $p_1 = p_2$ vs. H_a: $p_1 \neq p_2$; $P = 0.6981$ — insufficient evidence to reject H_0.

12.28 H_0: $p_1 = p_2$ vs. H_a: $p_1 \neq p_2$; $P = 0.9805$ — insufficient evidence to reject H_0.

12.29 (a) H_0: $p_1 = p_2$ vs. H_a: $p_1 > p_2$; $P = 0.0335$ — reject H_0 (at the 5% level). (b) −0.0053 to 0.2336.

12.30 (a) 0.1626 to 0.2398. (b) Zero does not lie in the 99% confidence interval for $p_2 - p_1$, so we would reject H_0: $p_2 - p_1 = 0$ in favor of the two-sided alternative at the 1% level. (c) Yes — $P < 0.00002$.

12.31 The population-to-sample ratio is large enough, and the smallest count is 10 — twice as big as it needs to be to allow the z procedures. Fatal heart attacks: $z = -2.67, P = 0.0076$. Non-fatal heart attacks: $z = -4.58, P < 0.000005$. Strokes: $z = 1.43, P = 0.1525$. The proportions for both kinds of heart attacks were significantly different; the stroke proportions were not.

12.32 (a) 0.2465 to 0.3359 — since 0 is not in this interval, we would reject H_0: $p_1 = p_2$ at the 1% level (in fact, P is practically 0). (b) No: $t = -0.8658$, which gives a P-value close to 0.4.

12.33 (a) −9.91% to −4.09%. Since 0 is not in this interval, we would reject H_0: $p_1 = p_2$ at the 1% level. (b) −0.7944 to −0.4056. Since 0 is not in this interval, we would reject H_0: $\mu_1 = \mu_2$ at the 1% level.

12.34 (a) $\hat{p}_1 = 0.1415, \hat{p}_2 = 0.1667; P = 0.6981$. (b) $P = 0.0336$. (c) From (a): −0.1056 to 0.1559. From (b): 0.001278 to 0.049036. The larger samples make the margin of error (and thus the length of the confidence interval) smaller.

CHAPTER REVIEW

12.35 No — the data is not based on an SRS, and thus the z procedures are not reliable in this case. In particular, a voluntary response sample is typically biased.

12.36 No — $\hat{p} = 49.19\%$, $z = 0.1834$, and $P = 0.4272$.

12.37 92.3% to 93.7%.

12.38 (a) −0.1965 to −0.0210. (b) Yes — 0 falls outside the confidence interval. In fact, $P = 0.0105$.

12.39 (a) No — $P = 0.1849$. (b) Yes — $P = 0.0255$. (c) The population is (presumably) very large, so the ratio of population-to-sample is big enough. Also, all the counts — 45 and 29 in (a); 21, 7, 24, and 22 in (b) — are bigger than 5. The counts for baseball players are too small.

12.40 (a) The numbers are percentages of total revenues, not percentages of businesses in the sample. Specifically, for each business, a variable ("percentage of revenues from highly regulated businesses") was measured, and the average of these values was computed. (b) Use the t procedures from Chapter 11 (we would also need to know the standard deviations).

Inference for Tables: Chi–Square Procedures

13

SECTION 13.1

13.1 (a) $P(X_2^2 > 1.41) = .4941$. (b) $P(X_9^2 > 19.62) = .0204$.

13.2 H_0: The distribution of colors of M&M's is the same as the distribution of colors advertised by the Mars/M&M Company. H_a: The distribution of colors of M&M's is different from the distribution of colors advertised by the Mars/M&M Company.

13.3 (a) H_0: The marital-status distribution of 25 to 29 year old U.S. males is the same as that of the population as a whole. H_a: The marital-status distribution of 25- to 29-year-old U.S. males is different from that of the population as a whole. (b) Expected counts: 116.3, 301.55, 35, and 47.15. (c) $X^2 = 250.24$, d.f. = 3. (d) P-value = $5.8 \times 10^{-54} = .0000$. Reject H_0. The two distributions are different.

13.4 H_0: The ethnicity distribution of the Ph.D. degree in 1994 is the same as it was in 1981. H_a: The ethnicity distribution of the Ph.D. degree in 1994 is different from the distribution in 1981. The expected values are 300 times the 1981 percents. We entered the observed counts in list L_1, the expected counts in L_2, and stored the calculated values of the difference terms $(O - E)^2/E$ in L_3.

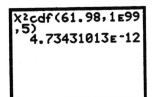

The test statistic is the sum of the difference terms in L_3: $X^2 = \Sigma(O - E)^2/E = 61.98$, and the degrees of freedom are $n - 1 = 5$. The P-value is $4.73 \times 10^{-23} = .0000$. We reject H_0 and conclude that the ethnicity distribution of the Ph.D. degree has changed from 1981 to 1994. (b) The greatest change is that many more nonresident aliens than expected received the degree in 1994 over the 1981 figures. To a lesser extent, a smaller proportion of white, non-Hispanics received the degree in 1994.

13.5 H_0: The age-group distribution in 1996 is the same as the 1980 distribution. H_a: The age-group distribution in 1996 is different from the 1980 distribution. One simulation produced observed counts: 37, 35, 15, 13. The expected counts: 41.39, 27.68, 19.64, and 11.28 are stored in list L_4, and the difference terms $(O - E)^2/E$ are assigned to L_5.

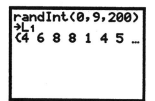

Note that none of the difference terms is very large. The test statistic is $X^2 = 3.76$, d.f. $= 3$, and the P-value $= .2886$. There is insufficient evidence to conclude that the distributions are different. The results of this simulation differ from those in the text; the reason may be due to different sample sizes or simply chance.

13.6 H_0: The distribution of digits, 0–9, is uniform. H_a: The distribution of digits is not uniform. The TI-83 command is: `randInt(0, 9, 200)` $\rightarrow L_1$. Here is the histogram for our calculator simulation (yours will be different). The observed counts are: 16, 20, 16, 20, 22, 22, 24, 18, 24, and 18. The expected counts are 200/10 = 20 for each digit. The observed counts are entered in L_2, the expected counts in L_3, and the calculated difference terms $(O - E)^2/E$ are assigned to L_4.

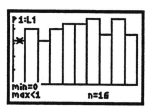

Not surprisingly, the difference terms are all fairly small. The degrees of freedom are $n - 1 = 9$, and $X^2 = 4$. The P-value is $P(X_5^2 > 4) = .55$. There is no evidence that the distribution of digits is not uniform.

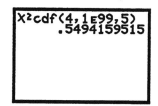

Theoretically, the 10 bars in the histogram should all be the same height; that they are not cannot be attributed to anything other than chance variation.

13.7 Exercise 13.6 is very similar. You should be surprised if you get a significant P-value. H_0: The die is fair ($p_1 = p_2 = \ldots = p_6 = 1/6$). H_a: The die is not fair. Use the command `randInt(1, 6, 300)` $\rightarrow L_1$ to simulate rolling a fair die 300 times. In our simulation, we obtained the following frequency distribution:

Side	1	2	3	4	5	6
Freq.	57	46	55	54	45	43

The expected counts under H_0: (300)(1/6) = 50 for each side. The test statistic is $X^2 = .98 + .32 + .5 + .32 + .5 + .98 = 3.6$, and the degrees of freedom are $n - 1 = 5$. The P-value is $P(X_5^2 > 3.6) = .608$. Since the P-value is large, we fail to reject H_0. There is no evidence that the die is not fair.

13.8

Outcome	H	T
Frequency	48	152
Expected	100	100

H_0: The distribution of heads and tails from spinning a 1982 penny shows equally likely outcomes. H_a: Heads and tails are not equally likely. d.f. = 1 and $X^2 = 27.04 + 27.04 = 58.08$. The P-value is $P(X_1^2 > 58.08) = 1.925(10)^{-13} = .0000$. Reject H_0 and conclude that spinning a 1982 penny does not produce equally likely results.

13.9 Let $p_1, p_2, \ldots, p_6$ denote the probability of getting a 1, 2, 3, ..., 6. If the die is fair, then $p_1 = p_2 = \ldots = p_6$. H_0: $p_1 = p_2 = \ldots = p_6$ (die is fair). H_a: The die is "loaded"/unfair. The observed counts for sides $1 - 6$ are: 26, 36, 39, 30, 38, 32. The expected counts are $(200)(1/6) = 33.33$ for each side. d.f. = $6 - 1 = 5$, and $X^2 = 1.612 + 0.214 + 0.965 + 0.333 + 0.654 + 0.053 = 3.831$. The P-value is $P(X_5^2 > 3.831) = .574$. Since this P-value is rather large, we fail to reject H_0, and conclude that there is no evidence that the die is "loaded."

13.10 The observed and expected values are:

Flavor	Grape	Lemon	Lime	Orange	Strawberry
Observed	530	470	420	610	585
Expected	523	523	523	523	523

H_0: Trix flavors are uniformly distributed. H_a: The flavors are not uniformly distributed. d.f. = $5 - 1 = 4$, and $X^2 = .09369 + 5.3709 + 20.285 + 14.472 + 7.3499 = 47.57$. $P(X_4^2 > 47.57) = 1.16(10)^{-9} = .0000$. Reject H_0 and conclude that either the Trix flavors are *not* uniformly distributed, or our box of Trix is not a *random* sample.

13.11 Answers will vary.

13.12 Since the wheel is divided into four equal parts, if it is in balance, then the four outcomes should occur with approximately equal frequency. Here are the observed and expected values:

Parts	I	II	III	IV
Observed	95	105	135	165
Expected	125	125	125	125

H_0: The wheel is balanced (the four outcomes are uniformly distributed). H_a: The wheel is not balanced. d.f. = 3 and $X^2 = 7.2 + 3.2 + 0.8 + 12.8 = 24$. The P-value is $P(X_3^2 > 24) = 2.5(10)^{-5} = .000025$. Reject H_0 and conclude that the wheel is not balanced. Since Part IV: Win nothing shows the greatest deviation from the expected result, there may be reason to suspect that the carnival game operator may have tampered with the wheel to make it harder to win.

SECTION 13.2

13.13 (a) 2 × 3. (b) 55.0%, 74.7%, and 37.5%. Some (but not too much) time spent in extracurricular activities seems to be beneficial. (c) On page 141 (top). (d) On page 141 (bottom). (e) The first and last columns have lower numbers than we expect in the "passing" row (and higher numbers in the "failing" row), while the middle column has this reversed — more passed than we would expect if all proportions were equal.

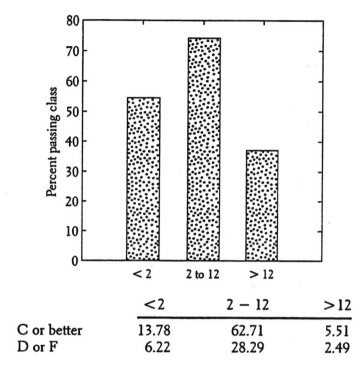

	< 2	2 − 12	> 12
C or better	13.78	62.71	5.51
D or F	6.22	28.29	2.49

13.14 (a) 3 × 2. (b) 22.5%, 18.6%, and 13.9%. A student's likelihood of smoking increases when one parent smokes, and increases even more when both smoke. (c) See Exercise 4.39. (d) The null hypothesis says that parents' smoking habits have no effect on their children. (e) Below. (f) In column 1, row 1, the expected count is much smaller than the actual count; meanwhile, the actual count is lower than expected in the lower left. This agrees with what we observed before: Children of non-smokers are less likely to smoke.

	Student smokes	Student does not smoke
Both parents smoke	332.49	1447.51
One parent smokes	418.22	1820.78
Neither parent smokes	253.29	1102.71

13.15 (b) $P = 0.0313$. Rejecting H_0 means that we conclude that there is a relationship between hours spent in extracurricular activities and performance in the course. (c) The highest contribution comes from column 3, row 2 (" > 12 hours of extracurricular activities, D or F in the course"). Too much time spent on these activities seems to hurt academic performance. (d) No — this study demonstrates association, not causation. Certain types of students may tend to spend a moderate amount of time in extracurricular activities and also work hard on their classes — one does not necessarily cause the other.

13.16 (b) P is essentially 0. By rejecting H_0, we conclude that there is a relationship between parents' smoking habits and those of their children. (c) The highest contributions come from C1 R1 ("both parents smoke, student smokes") and C1 R3 ("neither parent smokes, student smokes"). When both parents smoke, their student is much more likely to smoke; when neither parent smokes, their student is unlikely to smoke. (d) No — this study demonstrates association, not causation. There may be other factors (heredity or environment, for example) that cause both student and parent(s) to smoke.

13.17 (a) $(r-1)(c-1) = (2-1)(3-1) = 2$. (b) $X^2 = 6.926$ lies between 5.99 and 7.38; therefore, P is between 0.05 and 0.025.

13.18 (a) $(r-1)(c-1) = (3-1)(2-1) = 2$. (b) $X^2 = 37.568$ lies above 15.20 (the largest value in that row); therefore, $P < 0.0005$.

13.19 (a) and (b) Table below. 25% (2 out of 8) of the expected counts are less than 5, which goes against our guidelines. (c) 3 d.f.; P-value is between 0.0025 and 0.001 (in fact, $P = 0.0018$). (d) Students with high goals show a higher proportion of passing grades than those who merely wanted to pass.

	Actual ≥C	Actual D/F	Expected ≥C	Expected D/F
Wanted ≥ C	5	9	9.65	4.35
Wanted ≥ B	41	23	44.10	19.90
Wanted an A	27	3	20.67	9.33
Wanted an "A+"	9	2	7.58	3.42

13.20 (a) 2.96%, 13.07%, and 6.36%. (b) and (c) Table below — actual counts above, expected counts below. Expected counts are all greater than 5, so the chi-square test is safe. (d) H_0: there is no relationship between a member complaining and leaving the HMO vs. H_a: there is some relationship. 2 d.f.; $P < 0.0005$ (basically 0). (e) Members who file complaints — especially medical complaints — are more likely to leave the HMO.

	No complaint	Medical complaint	Non-medical complaint
Stayed	721 / 702.14	173 / 188.06	412 / 415.80
Left	22 / 40.86	26 / 10.94	28 / 24.20

13.21 (a) 7.01%, 14.02%, and 13.05%. (b) and (c) Table below — actual counts above, expected counts below. Expected counts are all much bigger than 5, so the chi-square test is safe. H_0: there is no relationship between worker class and race vs. H_a: there is some relationship. (d) 2 d.f.; $P < 0.0005$ (basically 0). (e) Black female child-care workers are more likely to work in non-household or preschool positions.

	Black	Other
Household	172 / 242.36	2283 / 2212.64
Non-household	167 / 117.58	1024 / 1073.42
Teachers	86 / 65.06	573 / 593.94

13.22 (a) $H_0: p_1 = p_2$ vs. $H_a: p_1 \neq p_2$. $z = -0.5675$ and $P = 0.5704$. (b) Table on page 143. $X^2 = 0.322$, which equals z^2. With 1 d.f., Table E tells us that $P > 0.25$; a statistical calculator gives $P = 0.5704$. (c) Gastric freezing is not significantly more (or less) effective than a placebo treatment.

	Improved	Did not improve
Gastric freezing	28	54
	29.73	52.28
Placebo	30	48
	28.27	49.72

13.23 (a) H_0: $p_1 = p_2$ vs. H_a: $p_1 < p_2$. The z test must be used because the chi-square procedure will not work for a one-sided alternative. (b) $z = -2.8545$ and $P = 0.0022$. Reject H_0; there is strong evidence in favor of H_a.

13.24 (a) $X^2 = 14.863$ with 2 d.f.; $P = 0.0006$, so reject H_0. Newark has a relatively high percentage (57.5%), Camden is very low (28.7%), and South Chicago falls in the middle (44.9%). (b) The data should come from independent SRSs of the (unregulated) child-care providers in each city.

13.25 H_0: all proportion are equal vs. H_a: some proportions are different. Table below. $X^2 = 10.619$ with 2 d.f.; and $P = 0.0049$ — good evidence against H_0, so we conclude that contact method makes a difference in response.

	Yes	No
Phone	168	632
One-on-one	200	600
Anonymous	224	576

13.26 (a) Yes, the evidence is *very* strong that a higher proportion of men die ($X^2 = 332.205$, 1 d.f.). Possibly many sacrificed themselves out of a sense of chivalry ("women and children first"). (b) For women, $X^2 = 103.767$ (2 d.f.) — a very significant difference. Over half of the lowest-status women died, but this percentage drops sharply when we look at middle-status women, and it drops again for high-status women. (c) For men, $X^2 = 34.621$ (2 d.f.) — another very significant difference (though not quite so strong as the women's value). Men with the highest status had the highest proportion surviving (over one-third). The proportion for low-status men was only about half as big, while middle-class men fared worst (only 12.8% survived).

13.27 (a) No; $X^2 = 1.051$ with 2 d.f., which gives $P = 0.5913$. (b) ABC News: $z = -0.7698$; $P = 0.4414$ (not significant). USA Today/CNN: $z = -5.1140$; P is essentially 0 (significant). New York Times/ CBS: $z = -4.4585$; P is essentially 0 (significant). (c) An individual test will be wrong for only 5% of all samples. Imagine doing three tests in a row: Assuming the first test comes out correct (which it does 95% of the time), there is still a 5% chance that the next test will come out wrong, etc. Altogether, all three will be correct only 85.7% ($= 0.95^3$) of the time.

CHAPTER REVIEW

13.28 The observed frequencies of scores in this sample, their marginal percents, and the expected numbers were:

Score	5	4	3	2	1
Frequency	167	158	101	79	30
Percent	31.2	29.5	18.9	14.8	5.6
Expected	81.855	117.7	132.68	105.93	96.835

H_0: The distribution of scores in this sample is the same as the distribution of scores for all students who took this inaugural exam. H_a: The distribution of scores in this sample is different from the national results. The degrees of freedom are $n - 1 = 4$, and the chi-square statistic is $X^2 = 88.57 + 13.80 + 7.56 + 6.85 + 46.13 = 162.9$. The P-value is $P(X_4^2 > 162.9) = 3.49(10)^{-34} = .0000$. Reject H_0 and conclude that the distribution of AP Statistics exam scores in this sample is different from the national distribution.

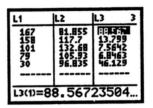

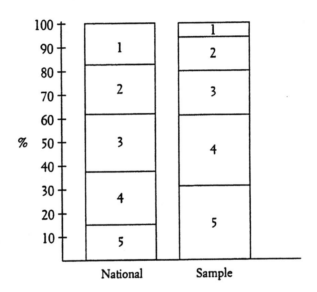

Postscript: As soon as the exam grades were sent to the students and their schools, in July 1997, several AP Statistics teachers who were subscribers to an AP Statistics discussion group on the Internet posted their grades in the spirit of sharing the results with their fellow teachers. While this was of interest to many of the pioneering AP Statistics teachers in their first year teaching this new course, this sample was a voluntary response sample, not a random sample. It should come as no surprise that these self-reported results were weighted toward the higher scores.

13.29 Using `randInt(0, 9, 200)` → L4, we obtained these counts for digits 0 to 9: 19, 17, 23, 22, 19, 20, 25, 12, 27, 16. $X^2 = 8.9$, d.f. = 9, P-value = .447. There is no evidence that the sample data were generated from a distribution that is different from the uniform distribution.

13.30 (a) $X^2 = 10.827$ (3 d.f.); $P = 0.0127$, which is significant at the 5% level, so we reject H_0. (b) Graph and table on page 145. The biggest difference between women and men is in Administration: A higher percentage of women chose this major. Meanwhile, a greater proportion of men chose other fields, especially Finance. (c) The largest chi-square components are the two from the "Administration" row. Many more women than we expect (91 actual, 76.36 expected) chose this major, while only 40 men chose this (54.64 expected). (d) The "Economics" row had expected counts of 6.41 and 4.59, respectively. Only the second number is less than 5, which is only one eighth (12.5%) of the counts in the table — the chi-square procedure is acceptable. (e) 386 responded, so 46.54% did not respond.

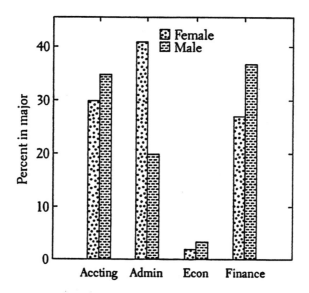

	Female	Male
Accounting	30.22%	34.78%
Administration	40.44%	24.84%
Economics	2.22%	3.73%
Finance	27.11%	36.65%

13.31 $X^2 = 3.277$ (4 d.f.); $P = 0.4874$, so we can accept H_0: all types of companies had the same response rate.

	Response	Nonresponse
Metal Products	17	168
Machinery	35	266
Electrical Equipment	75	477
Transportation Equipment	15	85
Precision Instruments	12	78

13.32 (a) $H_0: p_1 = p_2$, where p_1 and p_2 are the proportions of women customers in each city. $\hat{p}_1 = 0.8423$, $\hat{p}_2 = 0.6881$, $z = 3.9159$, and $P = 0.00009$. (b) $X^2 = 15.334$, which equals z^2. With 1 d.f., Table E tells us that $P < 0.0005$; a statistical calculator gives $P = 0.00009$. (c) 0.0774 to 0.2311.

13.33 4 degrees of freedom; $P > 0.25$ (in fact, $P = 0.4121$). There is not enough evidence to reject H_0 at any reasonable level of significance; the difference in the two income distributions is not statistically significant.

13.34 (a) This is a 4 × 4 table, so there are 9 d.f. (b) $X^2 = 256.8$ (3 d.f.); P is essentially 0. The highest response rates occur from September to mid-April; the lowest occur in the summer months, when more people are likely to be on vacation (that is when the "No answer" percentage is highest).

13.35 H_0: all refusal proportions are equal. The smallest expected count is 81.67, so the chi-square test is safe. $X^2 = 11.106$ (3 d.f.) and $P = 0.0112$ — pretty strong evidence against H_0. The two largest components of X^2 are the July–Aug refusals (which were higher than expected) and the Jan–April refusals (which were low). Perhaps more people had "other things to do" in the summer, and had less pressing business during the winter.

	Refused	Other
Jan 1–Apr 13	67	1491
	81.67	1476.33
Apr 21–June 20	86	1503
	83.29	1505.71
July 1–Aug 31	135	1940
	108.77	1966.23
Sept 1–Dec 1	124	2514
	138.28	2499.72

13.36 (a) $X^2 = 2.186$ (1 d.f.); $P = 0.1393$ — the difference is not statistically significant. (b) For "good condition" patients, $X^2 = 0.289$, while for "poor condition" patients, $X^2 = 0.019$ (both with 1 d.f.) — neither of these indicate significant differences ($P = 0.5909$ and 0.8904, respectively). (c) Though the effects are not statistically significant, Simpson's paradox is evident in that the P-value for the combined data is considerably lower than either of the P-values for the separate data.

13.37 (a) 0.5432 to 0.5968. (b) No: $z = 0.4884$, $P = 0.6253$. Or, using the exact counts (527/924 national, 96/174 student), $z = 0.4548$, $P = 0.6492$ — again, not at all significant. (c) Yes: $z = 7.9215$, P is essentially 0. (d) Yes: $X^2 = 13.847$ with 2 d.f.; $P < 0.001$. Both student groups were less likely to believe that the military was censoring the news.

	Yes	No
National	702	222
	675.37	248.63
Student Grp 1	117	57
	127.18	46.82
Student Grp 2	129	70
	145.45	53.55

13.38 (a) The null hypothesis would say that there is no relationship between rows and columns; this would mean, for example, that knowing a certain substance causes cancer in mice tells us nothing about whether or not it causes cancer in rats. (b) Agreement between mice and rats means high numbers in the upper left and lower right, and low numbers in the other two entries. When we check for "agreement" of two proportions using a chi-square test, we might expect to see (for example) high numbers in the first column and low numbers in the second column, or vice versa. (c) Mice and rats agree on 84.7% (211/249) chemicals. 84.1% (111/132) of chemicals that test positive for mice also get a + from rats, while 85.5% (100/117) of chemicals that test negative for mice also get a − from rats.

14

Inference for Regression

SECTION 14.1

14.1 (a) See Exercise 3.13 for scatterplot. $r = 0.99415$ and $\hat{y} = -3.660 + 1.19690x$. The scatterplot shows a strong linear relationship, which is confirmed by r. (b) β represents how much increase we can expect in humerus length when femur length increases by 1 cm. b (the estimate of β) is 1.1969; $a = -3.660$. (c) The residuals are -0.82262, -0.36682, 3.04248, -0.94202, and -0.91102; the sum is 0. $s = \sqrt{3.92843} = 1.9820$.

14.2 (a) See Exercise 3.37 for scatterplot. $r = 0.99899$ and $\hat{y} = 1.76608 + 0.080284x$. The scatterplot shows a strong linear relationship; steps per second seem to increase steadily with speed. (b) The residuals are 0.0106220, -0.0012674, -0.0010433, -0.0109613, -0.0093443, 0.0031464, and 0.0088482; the sum is 0.0000003. (c) $a = 1.766080$, $b = 0.080284$, and $s = \sqrt{0.000082236} = 0.0090684$.

14.3 (a) The regression equation is $\hat{y} = 8.003 + .0000662x$, where x = number of jet skis in use and $\hat{y}$ is the predicted number of fatalities. The sum of the residuals is $9.61 \times 10^{-7} \approx 0$. (b) The sum of the squares of residuals is 449.842737. $s = \sqrt{(\Sigma(\text{resid.})^2/(n-2))} = \sqrt{(449.842737)/8} = 7.4987$. (c) 8.003 is an estimate for α; .0000662 is an estimate for β; and 7.4987 estimates σ.

14.4 Using a $t(14)$ distribution: $0.188999 \pm (1.761)(0.004934) = 0.1803$ to 0.1977.

14.5 Using a $t(10)$ distribution: $0.687747 \pm (2.228)(0.2300) = 0.1753$ to 1.2002. β is the increase in second-round score we expect based on an increase of one shot in round one.

14.6 (a) $\hat{y} = -3.6596 + 1.1969$. (b) $t = \frac{1.1969}{0.0751} = 15.94$. (c) 3 d.f.; $P < 0.001$.

14.7 (a) $H_0: \beta = 0$, $H_a: \beta > 0$ (positive slope). (b) The t-statistics value is $t = 7.26$, d.f. $= n - 2 = 8$, P-value $= 4.38 \times 10^{-5} \cong .0000438$. (c) There is strong evidence to reject $H_0: \beta = 0$, in favor of H_a: The slope of the true regression line is positive. There is very strong evidence that as the number of jet skis in use increases, the number of fatalities also increases.

14.8 (a) r^2 is very close to 1, which means that nearly all the variation in steps per second is accounted for by foot speed. Also, the P-value for β is small. (b) β (the slope) is this rate; the estimate is listed as the coefficient of "Speed." 0.080284. Using a $t(5)$ distribution: $0.080284 \pm (4.032)(0.0016) = 0.07383$ to 0.08674.

14.9 (a) The plot on page 148 shows a strong positive linear relationship. (b) β (the slope) is this rate; the estimate is listed as the coefficient of "year": 9.31868. (c) 11 d.f.; $t^* = 2.201$; $9.31868 \pm (2.201)(0.3099) = 8.6366$ to 10.0008.

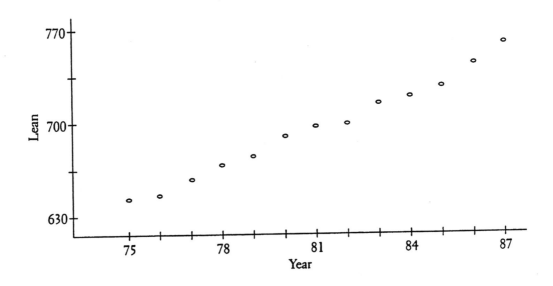

SECTION 14.2

14.10 (a) $\hat{y} = 8.65$ hundred cubic feet per day; savings: 115 ("1.15 hundred") ft³/day. (b) Use the prediction interval: 7.8767 to 9.4217. (c) Use the confidence interval: 8.3882 to 8.9101.

14.11 (a) Powerboat registrations is explanatory. (b) The plot shows a moderately strong positive linear relationship; there are no clear outliers or strongly influential points. (c) $r^2 = 88.6\%$ indicates that much, but not all, of the variation in manatee deaths is explained by powerboat registrations. (d) β is the number of additional manatee deaths we can expect when there are 1000 additional powerboat registrations. Using a $t(12)$ distribution: $0.12486 \pm (1.782)(0.01290) = 0.1019$ to 0.1478. (e) $\hat{y} = 45.972$ (about 46 manatee deaths per year). (f) Use the confidence interval: 41.49 to 50.46.

14.12 Use $t^* = 1.782$ from part (d), and $SE_{\hat{\mu}} = 2.06$: $45.97 \pm (1.782)(2.06) = 42.30$ to 49.64.

SECTION 14.3

14.13 (a) The stemplot does not show any *major* asymmetry, and also has no particular outliers. (b) The plot does not suggest a nonlinear relationship. There is *some* indication that there may be less variation at the high and low ends of the plot, but nothing too strong — there are too few observations to make any judgments about that.

```
-0 | 7
-0 |
-0 | 33
-0 | 110
 0 | 0011111
 0 | 2
 0 | 4
 0 | 6
```

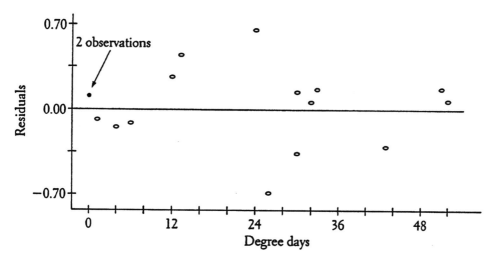

14.14 The number of points is so small that it is hard to judge much from the stemplot. The scatterplot of residuals vs. year does not suggest any problems. The regression in Exercise 14.9 should be fairly reliable.

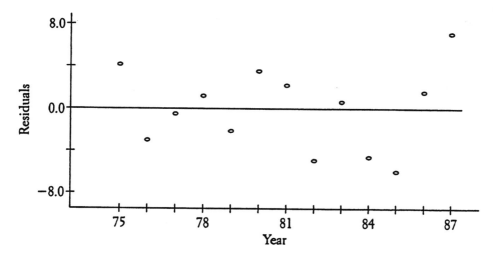

CHAPTER REVIEW

14.15 (a) See Exercise 3.46 for scatterplot. (b) $r^2 = 0.324$; $r = \sqrt{0.324} = 0.569$ — use the *positive* square root since the relationship is clearly positive, and r must have the same sign as b. (In fact, $r = 0.56896$.) The regression of overseas returns on U.S. returns explains about 1/3 (32.4%) of the variation in overseas returns; the relationship is positive. There is one outlier (in 1986) and one potentially influential point (in 1974). (c) $H_0: \beta = 0$ vs. $H_a: \beta \neq 0$; $t = 3.09$, and $P = 0.006$ (so we reject H_0). (d) $\hat{y} = 21.037$ percent.

(e) Use the prediction interval: -21.97 to 64.04 percent. In practice, this is of little value — the interval includes everything from a 20% loss to a 60% gain.

14.16 Use $t^* = 2.977$ from a $t(14)$ distribution: $8.6492 \pm (2.977)(0.1216) = 8.287$ to 9.011.

14.17 (a) It appears that the variation about the line is greater for larger values of x — on the left side of the plot, the residuals are less spread out. (b) Stemplot below (residuals were rounded to whole numbers first).

```
-2 | 54310
-1 | 75
-0 | 88732
 0 | 01
 1 | 03669
 2 | 36
 3 |
 4 |
 5 | 0
```

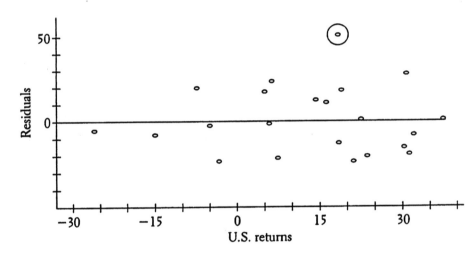

14.18 (a) and (b) See Exercise 3.55 for the plot; the influential points are the three in the upper right. (c) $H_0: \beta = 0$ vs. $H_a: \beta \neq 0$. $t = 4.28$, d.f. $= 15$, $P = 0.001$ (actually, $P < 0.001$). (Based on the statement, it might be reasonable to say that H_a is $\beta > 0$, a one-sided alternative, which would only make the P-value half as large.) (d) Franklin's predicted income was $\hat{y} = 21.6$ million dollars; the residual is -7.8. (e) Use the prediction interval: -30.96 to 74.17. Franklin's actual income seems quite reasonable when compared to this wide interval; we would not have been able to predict Franklin's problems from this.

14.19 (a) $\hat{y} = 26.3320 + (0.687747)(89) = 87.5415$ (using the output of Figure 14.5), residual $= 6.4585$. (b) $\Sigma\text{residual}^2 = 356.885$; $s = \sqrt{\frac{1}{10}(356.885)} = \sqrt{35.6885} = 5.974$.

14.20 (a) $r = \sqrt{\text{"R squared"}} = \sqrt{0.472} = 0.687$ — use the *positive* square root since r must have the same sign as b. (b) $P = 0.0136$ (taken from Figure 14.5). (c) $P = \frac{1}{2}(0.0136) = 0.0068$.

14.21 Take $t^* = 2.145$ from a $t(14)$ distribution: $1.0892 \pm (2.145)(0.1389) = 0.7913$ to 1.3871.

14.22 (a) $\bar{x} = 89.67$ and $s_x = 7.83$. (b) $x^* = 90$; $(x^* - \bar{x})^2 = 0.1089$. (c) $\Sigma(x - \bar{x})^2 = (11)(7.83)^2 = 674.4$. (d) $SE_\mu = (5.974)\sqrt{\frac{1}{12} + \frac{0.1089}{674.4}} = 1.7262$. (e) $\hat{y} = 88.23$; confidence interval: $88.23 \pm (2.228)(1.7262) = 84.38$ to 92.08.

14.23 (a) The heavy fish does not appear to be out of place on the width vs. length plot (on page 151). (However, when Minitab does the regression for (b), it notes that this fish has the largest residual.) (b) $\hat{y} = -0.8831 + 0.297518x$. (c) Based on Minitab output: $\hat{y} = 6.5549$; confidence interval is

$6.5549 \pm 0.1294 = 6.4255$ to 6.6842. This is based on $SE_{\hat{\mu}} = 0.0645$ and $t^* = 2.005$ from a $t(54)$ distribution. (d) A stemplot of the residuals (below) gives *some* suggestion of right-skewness, and has two moderate low outliers. A plot of residuals vs. length suggests that there may be more variability in width for larger lengths, but that may just be because we have few observations for small fish. There are no apparent gross violations, so inference should be fairly safe.

```
−1 | 0
−0 | 8
−0 |
−0 | 555544444
−0 | 3332222222
−0 | 111110000
 0 | 000000111
 0 | 22333
 0 | 444555
 0 | 666
 0 | 8
 1 | 0
 1 | 2
```

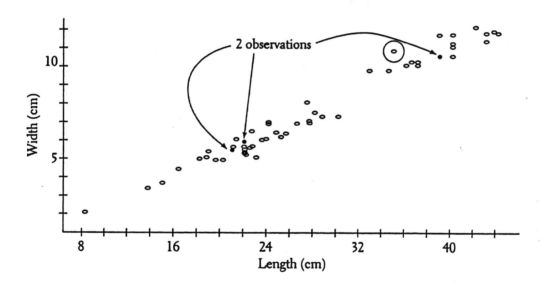

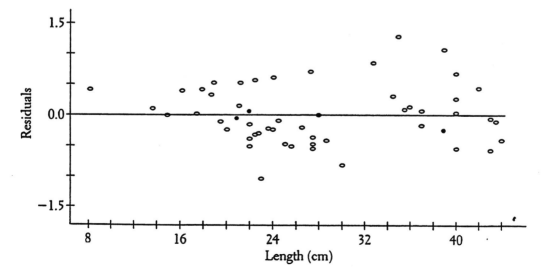

14.24 (a) The plot shows only a *very* slight pattern (weight increases with length). There is a definite outlier: fish #40, the "heavy fish" mentioned in the previous problem.

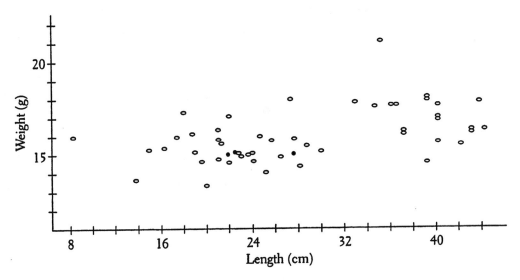

(b) We would expect weight to increase more-or-less linearly with volume — if we double volume, we double weight; if we triple the volume, we triple the weight, etc. When all dimensions (length, width, and height) are doubled, the *volume* of an object increases by a factor of $8 = 2^3$. Similarly, if we triple all dimensions, volume (and, approximately, weight) increases by a factor of $27 = 3^3$. It then makes sense that the cube root (i.e., the one-third power) of the weight increases at an approximately linear rate with length.

(c) The second plot omits the heavy fish — which would still be an outlier. It does not really look any more linear; there is still a lot of scatter that obscures any obvious patterns. There are no apparent outliers (except for the heavy fish).

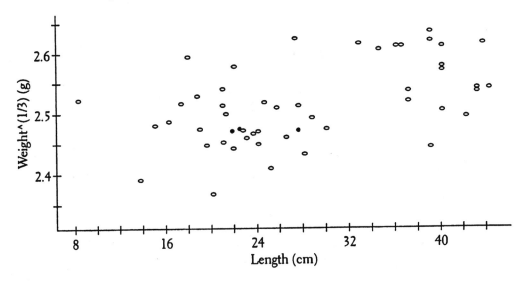

(d) There is very little change in appearance of the plots, or in r^2: using the original weight variable, $r^2 = 0.2346$; with weight$^{1/3}$, $r^2 = 0.2389$. In fact, if we omit the outlier from both computations, we actually find that r^2 *decreases*: 0.2515 before, 0.2502 after.

(e) If we use all the fish: $\hat{y} = 2.40306 + 0.0038135x$; $\hat{y} = 2.49839$ when $x = 25$; confidence interval: $2.49839 \pm t^*SE_\mu = 2.49839 \pm (2.005)(0.00870) = 2.48094$ to 2.51585.

Without fish #40: $\hat{y} = 2.40899 + 0.0034570x$; $\hat{y} = 2.49541$ when $x = 25$; confidence interval: $2.49541 \pm (2.006)(0.00772) = 2.47994$ to 2.51089. (f) Both the stemplot and the plot of residuals vs. length show no gross violations of the assumptions, except for the high outlier for fish #40; as we saw in part (e), however, omitting that fish makes little difference in our line.

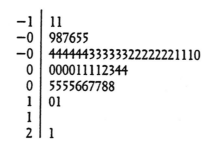

```
-1 | 11
-0 | 987655
-0 | 444444333333322222221110
 0 | 000011112344
 0 | 5555667788
 1 | 01
 1 |
 2 | 1
```

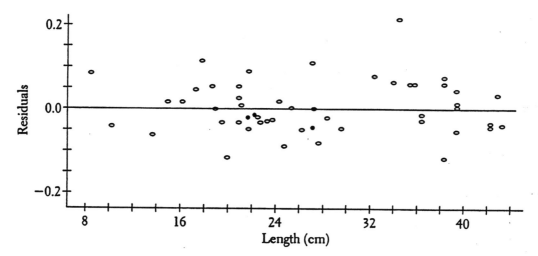

15

Analysis of Variance

SECTION 15.1

15.1 (a) The $F(2, 25)$ curve begins at $(0, 1)$ and decreases, approaching the x-axis asymptotically. (b) The $F(5, 50)$ curve begins near the origin, rises to a peak and then decreases, approaching the x-axis asymptotically. (c) $F(12, 100)$ reaches a higher peak, which is slightly to the right of the peak for $F(5, 50)$. (e) As the sample sizes increase, the F-distribution curve becomes more symmetric and more like a normal distribution.

15.2 (a) $F^* = 3.68$. (b) Not significant at either 10% or 5% (in fact, $P = 0.1166$).

15.3 (a) Significant at 5%, but not at 1%. (b) Between 0.02 and 0.05 ($P = 0.0482$).

15.4 $F = 10.57$; P-value (for the two-sided alternative) is between 0.02 and 0.05 ($P = 0.0217$) — so this is significant at 5% but not at 1%.

15.5 (a) H_0: $\sigma_{\text{skilled}} = \sigma_{\text{novice}}$ vs. H_a: $\sigma_s \neq \sigma_n$. (b) $F = 4.007$; P-value is between 0.05 and 0.10 ($P = 0.0574$).

15.6 (a) H_0: $\sigma_s = \sigma_n$ vs. H_a: $\sigma_s \neq \sigma_n$. (b) $F = 2.196$; P-value is greater than 0.20 ($P = 0.2697$).

15.7 $F = 2.242$; the $F(19, 9)$ distribution doesn't show up in the tables, but by comparing to the $F(20, 9)$ distribution we see that the P-value is greater than 0.20 ($P = 0.2152$). The difference is not significant.

15.8 $F = 1.5443$; the P-value is 0.3725, so the difference is not statistically significant.

SECTION 15.2

15.9 (a) The distribution for perch has an extreme high outlier (20.9); the bream distribution has a mild low outlier (12.0). Otherwise there is no strong skewness. (b) Bream: 12.0, 13.6, 14.1, 14.9, 15.5; Perch: 13.2, 15.0, 15.55, 16.675, 20.9; Roach: 13.3, 13.925, 14.65, 15.275, 16.1. The most important difference seems to be that perch are larger than the other two fish. It also appears that (typically) bream *may* be slightly smaller than roach.

```
Bream                 Perch                      Roach
12 | 0                12 |                       12 |
12 |                  12 |                       12 |
13 | 333344          13 | 2                     13 | 3
13 | 5677788889      13 | 69                    13 | 6799
14 | 111233          14 | 3                     14 | 0013
14 | 78899           14 | 55667889              14 | 677
15 | 001113          15 | 000000011112344       15 | 122344
15 | 5               15 | 56788999              15 | 6
16 |                 16 | 0112333               16 | 1
16 |                 16 | 8                     16 |
17 |                 17 | 003                   17 |
17 |                 17 | 56667789              17 |
18 |                 18 | 1                     18 |
18 |                 18 |                       18 |
19 |                 19 |                       19 |
19 |                 19 |                       19 |
20 |                 20 |                       20 |
20 |                 20 | 9                     20 |
```

15.10 (a) $H_0: \mu_1 = \mu_2 = \mu_3$ — the mean weights of the three types are equal. (b) $F = 29.92$ and $P < 0.001$. (c) Perch seem to be actually different in weight from the other two species; the mean weight of bream and roach may not differ greatly (the two confidence intervals overlap).

15.11 (a) Mean yields: 131.03, 143.15, 146.23, 143.07, 134.8. The mean yields first increase with plant density, then decrease; the greatest yield occurs at or around 20,000 plants per acre. (b) $H_0: \mu_1 = \mu_2 = \mu_3 = \mu_4 = \mu_5$ (all plant densities give the same mean yield per acre) vs. H_a: not all means are the same. (c) $F = 0.50$ and $P = 0.736$. The differences are not significant. (d) The sample sizes were small, which means there is a lot of potential variation in the outcome.

```
12,000          16,000          20,000          24,000          28,000
11 | 38          11 |            11 |            11 |            11 | 9
12 |             12 | 1          12 |            12 |            12 |
13 |             13 | 5          13 | 0          13 | 58         13 |
14 | 3           14 |            14 | 0          14 |            14 |
15 | 0           15 | 0          15 | 0          15 | 6          15 | 1
16 |             16 | 7          16 | 5          16 |            16 |
```

15.12 (a) I, the number of populations, is 3; the sample sizes from the 3 populations are $n_1 = 35$, $n_2 = 55$ (after discarding the outlier), and $n_3 = 20$; the total sample size is $N = 110$. (b) numerator ("factor"): $I - 1 = 2$, denominator ("error"): $N - I = 107$. (c) Since $F > 7.41$, the largest critical value for an $F(2,100)$ distribution in Table D, we conclude that $P < 0.001$.

15.13 (a) I, the number of populations, is 5; the sample sizes are $n_1 = 4$, $n_2 = 4$, $n_3 = 4$, $n_4 = 3$, and $n_5 = 2$; the total sample size is $N = 17$. (b) numerator ("factor"): $I - 1 = 4$, denominator ("error"): $N - I = 12$. (c) Since $F < 2.48$, the smallest critical value for an $F(4, 12)$ distribution in Table D, we conclude that $P > 0.100$.

15.14 (a) Populations: tomato varieties; response variable: yield. $I = 4$, $n_1 = n_2 = n_3 = n_4 = 10$, and $N = 40$; 3 and 36 d.f. (b) Populations: customers (responding to different package designs); response variable: attractiveness rating. $I = 6$, $n_1 = n_2 = n_3 = n_4 = n_5 = n_6 = 120$, and $N = 720$; 5 and 714 d.f.

(c) Populations: dieters (under different diet programs); response variable: weight change after six months. $I = 3$, $n_1 = n_2 = 10$, $n_3 = 12$, and $N = 32$; 2 and 29 d.f.

15.15 Yes: $\frac{\text{largest } s}{\text{smallest } s} = \frac{1.186}{0.770} = 1.54$.

15.16 Yes: $\frac{\text{largest } s}{\text{smallest } s} = \frac{22.27}{11.44} = 1.95$.

15.18 (a) The biggest difference is that single men earn considerably less than men who have been or are married. Widowed and married men earn the most; divorced men earn about $1,300 less (on the average), and single men are $4,000 below that. (b) Yes: $\frac{8119}{5731} = 1.42$. (c) 3 and 8231. (d) The sample sizes are so large that even small differences would be found to be significant; we have some fairly large differences. (e) No — single men are likely to be younger than men in the other categories. This means that typically they have less experience, and have been with their companies less time than the others, and so have not received as many raises, etc.

15.19 (a) H_0: $\mu_{r1} = \mu_{r2} = \mu_{r3}$ (all class rank means are same) vs. H_a: not all means are the same. (b) 2 and 253 (for all three tests). (c) Yes: $\frac{10.8}{10.5} = 1.03$, $\frac{1.31}{1.17} = 1.12$, and $\frac{55}{40} = 1.375$. Comparing to $F(2,200)$ critical values, we find $P_{\text{rank}} > 0.100$, P_{sem} is between 0.025 and 0.010, and $P_{\text{grade}} < 0.001$. (d) Mean high school class rank varies little between the groups. Regarding the other two variables, there appears to be little difference between the CS and Sci/Eng majors. However, "semesters of HS math" and "average grade in HS math" both show a significant difference between CS/Sci/Eng majors and those in the "Other" category: On the average, the first two groups had about one half-semester more math, and had grades about 0.25 higher.

15.20 (a) MSE $= \frac{1}{107}[(34)(0.770)^2 + (54)(1.186)^2 + (19)(0.780)^2] = \frac{107.67}{107} = 1.0063$; $s_p = \sqrt{\text{MSE}} = 1.003$. (b) Use $t^* = 1.984$ from a $t(100)$ distribution (since $t(107)$ is not available): $15.747 \pm t^* s_p / \sqrt{55} = 15.479$ to 16.015. Using software, we find that for a $t(107)$ distribution, $t^* = 1.982$; this rounds to the same interval.

15.21 $\bar{x} = \frac{1}{110}[(35)(14.131) + (55)(15.747) + (20)(14.605)] = 15.025$. MSG $= \frac{1}{2}[(35)(14.131 - 15.025)^2 + (55)(15.747 - 15.025)^2 + (20)(14.605 - 15.025)^2] = 30.086$. $F = \frac{30.086}{1.003} = 29.996$ — reasonably close to Minitab's output.

15.22 MSE $= \frac{1}{12}[(3)(18.09)^2 + (3)(19.79)^2 + (3)(15.07)^2 + (2)(11.44)^2 + (1)(22.27)^2] = \frac{3595.7}{12} = 299.64$ — this agrees with Minitab's output (except for roundoff error). $\bar{x} = \frac{1}{17}[(4)(131.03) + (4)(143.15) + (4)(146.23) + (3)(143.07) + (2)(134.75)] = 140.02$. MSG $= \frac{1}{4}[(4)(131.03 - 140.02)^2 + (4)(143.15 - 140.02)^2 + (4)(146.23 - 140.02)^2 + (3)(143.07 - 140.02)^2 + (2)(134.75 - 140.02)^2] = \frac{600.18}{4} = 150.04$.

15.23 Use $t^* = 1.782$ from a $t(12)$ distribution: 130.81 to 161.65.

CHAPTER REVIEW

15.24 (a) H_0: $\sigma_m = \sigma_w$ vs. H_a: $\sigma_m \neq \sigma_w$; $F = 1.16$, which gives $P = 0.3754$ (looking up values in Table D allows us to determine that $P > 0.2$). (b) No — F procedures are not robust against nonnormality, even with large samples.

15.25 (a) Populations: nonsmokers, moderate smokers, and heavy smokers; response variable: hours of sleep per night. $I = 3$, $n_1 = n_2 = n_3 = 200$, and $N = 600$; 2 and 597 d.f. (b) Populations: different concrete mixtures; response variable: strength. $I = 5$, $n_1 = \cdots = n_5 = 6$, and $N = 30$; 4 and 25 d.f. (c) Populations: teaching methods; response variable: test scores. $I = 4$, $n_1 = n_2 = n_3 = 10$, $n_4 = 12$, and $N = 42$; 3 and 38 d.f.

15.26 (a) The data suggest that the presence of too many nematodes reduces growth. Table and stemplots on page 157. (b) H_0: $\mu_1 = \cdots = \mu_4$ (all mean heights are the same) vs. H_a: not all means are the same. This ANOVA tests whether nematodes affect mean plant growth. (c) Minitab output is shown below. The first two levels (0 and 1000 nematodes) do not appear to be significantly different, nor do the last two. However, it does appear that somewhere between 1000 and 5000 nematodes, the tomato plants begin to feel the effects of the worms, and are hurt by their presence.

Nematodes	n_i	$\bar{x}_i$	s_i
0	4	10.650	2.053
1000	4	10.425	1.486
5000	4	5.600	1.244
10,000	4	5.450	1.771

```
        0              1000            5000           10,000

       3 |            3 |             3 |             3 | 2
       4 |            4 |             4 | 6           4 |
       5 |            5 |             5 | 04          5 | 38
       6 |            6 |             6 |             6 |
       7 |            7 |             7 | 4           7 | 5
       8 |            8 | 2           8 |             8 |
       9 | 12         9 |             9 |             9 |
      10 | 8         10 |            10 |            10 |
      11 |           11 | 113        11 |            11 |
      12 |           12 |            12 |            12 |
      13 | 5         13 |            13 |            13 |
```

Minitab output:
```
ANALYSIS OF VARIANCE
SOURCE      DF         SS          MS           F           P
FACTOR       3     100.65       33.55       12.08       0.001
ERROR       12      33.33        2.78


TOTAL       15     133.97


                            INDIVIDUAL 95 PCT CI'S FOR MEAN
                            BASED ON POOLED STDEV
LEVEL    N      MEAN     STDEV  ------+---------+---------+---------+
0        4    10.650     2.053                        (-------*------)
1000     4    10.425     1.486                        (-------*------)
5000     4     5.600     1.244  (------*-------)
10000    4     5.450     1.771  (------*------)
                                -----+---------+---------+-------+
POOLED STDEV =     1.667         5.0       7.5      10.0      12.5
```

15.27 The stemplots (on page 158) show that the Jaguar XJ12 and the Rolls-Royce Silver Spur are again low outliers, so we omit them. The Mercedes-Benz S420 and S500 are also somewhat low among large cars. However, they are not as extreme as the other two, so one might decide to keep them in.

Descriptive statistics follow the stemplots, appearing as slightly modified Minitab input (some of the statistics supplied by Minitab are not needed here). The variable "Large" includes the two Mercedes-Benz cars, while "Large2" does not. Finally, there are two ANOVAs: the first uses "Large"; the second uses "Large2."

In the first ANOVA, the test is significant at the 1% level; in the second, it is significant at the 5% level. Both sets of confidence intervals show some overlap, but suggest a conclusion similar to that for city mileage — the most important difference is that compact cars have better average mileage than the other two types.

	Compact		Midsize		Large
15		15	0	15	
16	0	16		16	
17		17		17	
18		18		18	
19		19		19	0
20		20		20	0
21		21		21	
22		22	0	22	
23		23	000	23	
24	0000	24	0	24	0
25	00	25	00	25	000
26	000	26	0000	26	000
27	000	27	00	27	00
28	0	28	0	28	00
29	00000	29	000	29	
30	0	30		30	
31	0	31	00	31	
32	00	32		32	
33	0	33		33	
34		34		34	
35	00	35		35	

Minitab output:

```
              N      MEAN    MEDIAN    STDEV      MIN       MAX       Q1        Q3
Compact      25    28.240    28.000    3.345   24.000    35.000   25.500    30.500
Midsize      19    26.316    26.000    2.689   22.000    31.000   24.000    29.000
Large        13    25.077    26.000    2.753   19.000    28.000   24.500    27.000
Large2       11    26.091    26.000    1.300   24.000    28.000   25.000    27.000
```

```
ANALYSIS OF VARIANCE
SOURCE      DF        SS        MS         F          p
FACTOR       2     94.55     47.28      5.21      0.009
ERROR       54    489.59      9.07
TOTAL       56    584.14
                                  INDIVIDUAL 95 PCT CI'S FOR MEAN
                                  BASED ON POOLED STDEV
LEVEL        N      MEAN     STDEV    ---+---------+---------+---------+---
Compact     25    28.240     3.345                        (-----*-----)
Midsize     19    26.316     2.689                 (------*------)
Large       13    25.077     2.753        (-------*--------)
                                     ---+---------+---------+---------+---
POOLED STDEV =     3.011           24.0      26.0      28.0      30.0
```

```
ANALYSIS OF VARIANCE
SOURCE    DF       SS      MS         F          p
FACTOR    2      55.26   27.63      3.46       0.039
ERROR     52    415.57    7.99
TOTAL     54    470.84

                                INDIVIDUAL 95 PCT CI'S FOR MEAN
                                BASED ON POOLED STDEV
LEVEL       N    MEAN    STDEV   --------+---------+---------+--------
Compact    25   28.240   3.345                      (------*-------)
Midsize    19   26.316   2.689        (-------*--------)
Large2     11   26.091   1.300     (----------*----------)
                                --------+---------+---------+--------
POOLED STDEV =   2.827            25.5      27.0      28.5
```

15.28 (a) $t = -0.34135$ with 12 d.f.; $P = 0.7387$. (b) $\bar{x} = 2.344$, MSG $= 0.02652$, MSE $= 0.25411$, and $F = 0.10436$; $P = 0.7491$. (c) The two P-values differ by about 0.01 — an unimportant difference in most cases.

15.29 Using the means and standard deviations from 15.26(a): $\bar{x} = \frac{1}{16}[(4)(10.650) + (4)(10.425) + (4)(5.600) + (4)(5.450)] = 8.031$; all other values can be confirmed from the Minitab output in 15.26. Table D places the P-value at less than 0.001; software gives $P = 0.0006$.